The Water Bearer Who Refused to Drown

Jordyn Osborne

IngramSpark

The Water Bearer Who Refused to Drown

Introduction

A water bearer is someone who carries water from one place to another. She is also the symbol attributed to Aquarius...the 11th sign of the Zodiac. According to lore, the water bearer not only pours out water, but also life-giving wisdom, mercy, and compassion.

While all that sounds lovely and wonderful, there is a catch...there's always a catch, right? At least in the story found in these pages. And the catch is that sometimes the compassion and mercy that flows so freely to others from her vessel can almost drown her if she's not careful. But there are so many other ways to drown as well. In addition to water, there is blood, vomit, bile, disease, solitude, medicine, noise, lies, betrayal, and so much more.

As you read this memoir, please know, only a very few liberties have been taken; however, the medical details, dialogue, and text messages are spot on. Some of the names have been changed and purposefully reselected to protect the innocent, as well as the not-so-innocent. I have told the truth in this memoir...mine and sometimes others, where the two intersected and deeply impacted my life. And now...*The Water Bearer Who Refused to Drown.*

For Gram, Dr A., Smith, and Thiny ~
You all have inspired me to live more, to do more, to be more.

Acknowledgments

Thank you to my amazing team of editors—Jeff Drummond, Taylor Drummond, Dr. Gary Grieve-Carlson, and Bradford Nicarry—for their hard work, amazing suggestions, and effort to make this memoir all that it is.

Thank you to my college volleyball coach-turned-friend, Wayne Perry, who inspired me to have the courage to write this book, after he published his own last year.

Thank you to kindred spirit and fellow writer, Nadia Bolz-Weber. Who, although she does not know me, gave me an unwitting stamp of approval to be this level of open in telling my story. Allowing others to see behind the curtain is no trip down the yellow brick road...there is always a threat of flying monkeys. So if you know the real Jordyn Osborne, well...here are a few bits of Oz you may not know.

Thank you to each friend who encouraged me to share my story and words with the world. Your enthusiasm spurred me to do exactly that.

Contents

Patriarchy, a Flooded Bathroom, and Unconditional Love

1

Chapter 1: Exiting Water, Entering Sugar

I took swimming lessons as a kid at my local YMCA for several years...so many years that I can still smell the aroma of chlorine that increased from the moment I entered the locker room until I opened the door to the pool. My grandpa also had an above ground pool in his backyard, so I spent plenty of summer afternoons becoming a shriveled prune with my sister and a neighbor kid. We had some pool toys...the usual suspects—small rafts, a floating basketball net and ball, and of course, the large, multi-colored, striped beach ball.

One summer evening, my mom, dad, sister, and I were having a family of friends over for swim time and a picnic in my grandpa's backyard. We were all in the pool when dark clouds rolled in, and within a few minutes, the thunder clapped loudly. We waited for the next clap, and then it was all over.

"Alright," Dad said, "everybody out of the pool until this blows over."

And so, we all lined up at the ladder, took our turns, and headed up the yard to the covered back porch. There were four girls–two sets of sisters–between the ages of 10 and 14, plus two sets of parents. We grabbed our towels to dry off and keep warm as a cool wind blew through.

We had forgotten to snag the beach ball that we were playing with in the pool. And within a few minutes of the sideways rain, loud thunder, and lightning that struck every 15 seconds or so, the ball had been blown out of the pool and was rushing towards the farmer's field behind the pool.

"Daddy!" I cried in my 12-year-old voice. "The beach ball is blowing away! Can you please go get it?"

My father looked at my face and then at the ball that was about 100 yards away, and finally, he looked up at the 30-foot tall trees that dotted my grandpa's backyard. He saw the disappointment on my face, but before he could say anything, my father's hunting buddy interjected.

"Jordyn, honey," Rodney started, "it's lightning out there."

And then Rodney said something I'd never forget.

"We can get you another ball, Jordyn, but we can't get you another daddy."

I stood there and thought about those words for several minutes, and Rodney was right. There was no sense in risking anyone's life for an inflatable beach ball. Lightning loves water, and tall things, like the half dozen trees in the yard, and possibly one single person standing in the middle of a field. So I sat down on the cement step to my grandpa's house, and I watched as the storm blew my beach ball out of sight.

September 17, 2021

It was an ordinary day in the middle of the COVID-19 pandemic, and by ordinary, I mean, Groundhog Day #558. I was working from home, plugging away on my laptop, and across the room, my partner of 7.5 years did the same. All the while, I was dreaming of the next day. It was to be my first public outdoor gathering since the CRUD made its presence known to the world at large. My pickleball crew in Phoenixville, PA, had planned an outdoor picnic and play day, and I for one could not wait. I had the heebie-jeebies from being cooped up for so very long, much like the rest of the world, I was guessing. So at lunchtime, I put the laptop down for a bit and headed to our small kitchen to prepare my offering for the picnic the next day.

I opened the can of pumpkin pie mix and dumped it into a medium-size bowl, along with two cups of powdered sugar and a block of cream cheese. This dip was so delicious, and although I might have been rushing pumpkin season a bit, I didn't care.

"Hey, I'm heading out to the post office for a few minutes," said Brennan as he passed by the kitchen on the way to the apartment door.

"Ok, I'll see you in a bit," I replied, while plugging in my electric hand mixer. The door closed behind him, and the next thing I remembered was waking up on the living room sofa when Brennan opened the front door 15 minutes later. I sat up, looked down at my shirt, which looked like a cocaine cutting board, and turned my head a bit to the left to half look at him.

"I made a mess," was all I could muster.

Brennan took a quick peek in the kitchen, only to find that every crack, crease, and crevice was filled with the aforementioned pumpkin, cream cheese, and powdered sugar. He did what he always did in strange, clearly-not-right, and/or crisis situations...he jumped into action. He began cleaning the entire kitchen from top to bottom, save the dent that the wheeled island made in the wall as I crashed into it. I apparently fell backwards into the island before I blacked out. Thankfully, the cord to the mixer was short and pulled out of the wall before it could do more damage than mess up the kitchen.

While Brennan cleaned, I fell in and out of consciousness. When I got up again, I walked over to the kitchen and said, "Hey, my tongue really hurts," sticking out my tongue for him to see.

"Yeah, you might need a stitch. Let's get you to Urgent Care," Brennan said as he examined my tongue. "You bit your tongue."

I stepped back, took a look in the mirrored wall hanging, and sure enough, there was a big gash on the right side of my tongue.

Within minutes, we were on our way to the Urgent Care, located about a mile down the road. Once inside, I waited for a few minutes before I was called back to be seen. After asking Brennan and me a few questions, the doctor had determined that I had most likely had a seizure, and possibly a few more mini-seizures after the main one.

"I'm going to send you to the ER," she said. "We're calling ahead to them so that they know you are coming. You won't have to wait as long that way."

And with that, we headed out again towards our apartment that was just one more mile to the hospital. Brennan pulled up to the front of the ER, dropped me off, parked, then came in to meet me, just as I had finished my paperwork. Within 10 minutes, a staff member called my name to go back. Brennan stayed with me until the time they were prepping me for a CT scan. We said our goodbyes, as we both decided it wasn't the best idea for him to stay in a waiting room full of people in the midst of CRUD-19.

"Text or call me after your scan," Brennan said. I nodded in agreement. We kissed, and with that, Brennan was headed home.

After another 20 minutes or so, they wheeled my gurney down the hall, around a few bends, and into a room to do the CT scan. I don't remember this scan, but I do remember when the attending doctor came back into my holding room. Holding...holding...holding onto hope, and to a faith I had not called upon in almost a decade. Suburban Philadelphia was not the hotbed of faithful followers like Lancaster County, PA. But there, in a cold, semi-sterile environment (because, well, CRUD-19), I prayed for the best, but I could never have prepared for what happened next.

"Hello, I'm Fred, the attending physician today," said the doctor who walked into my room. "I'm not quite sure how to say this," Fred began and then continued, "but you have a mass on your brain."

"Ummm, what?" I asked. Followed up by a quietly escaping, "F—," for which I should have apologized, but I was pretty sure he granted me a pass on my language in that moment. "Also, I'll need your driver's license," said Fred. "You won't be able to drive for six months due to the seizure." I closed my eyes and let the tears flow. This could NOT be happening.

I called Brennan to tell him the news. His response was similar to mine, along with, "I really wasn't expecting this…at all." We both thought I had passed out in the kitchen from low blood sugar. We were both wrong. So. Very. Wrong. Then I made a few calls to my immediate family, and texted some close friends as well.

News quickly spread to my extended family, friends, and friends of family and friends. Perfect (in the most wonderful way possible) strangers as well as loved ones prayed for me, as I had to wait overnight for an MRI to tell whether the tumor was malignant or benign. For reasons unknown to me, I was probably the calmest of everyone. Perhaps it was my brain and body's way of protecting me…perhaps it was all the thoughts and prayers…perhaps it was the realization that I couldn't do a damn thing about it.

The next morning, I went for the MRI earlier than they said, which suited me just fine—less time to worry. I wasn't thrilled about the idea of going through that small tube with the crazy knocks and noises that went on for about half an hour. But with the help of a Xanax and some Sarah McLachlan, it was much better than I imagined.

When the neurologist came in an hour or so later, I tensed up a bit. But a weight was lifted when he said "benign," "close to the surface," and "operable." He then told me what I had was known as a meningioma, the most common type of "head tumor." Technically, the tumor rested outside the gray matter, in a layer of the brain called the *meninges*.

"We want to send you downtown tonight to our big hospital to see a neurosurgeon," said the neurologist on duty. But, as I had been strictly instructed by a dear friend, who had seen more than her fair share of doctors, surgeons, and hospitals, no one was going to touch my brain except UPenn or Thomas Jefferson docs. So I quickly, but politely replied to him…

"Thanks, but I'm just going to go home tonight, and I will call tomorrow to get things lined up with a neurosurgeon."

Two hours later, Brennan picked me up and drove me back to our apartment. We sat down in our usual spots—his, the armless chair in the corner, and mine, the sofa. For 8.5 years, we had assumed these positions every night that he hadn't had his son. We had played countless games of ten different versions of Trivial Pursuit from these spots. We had listened to music from these seats...great music that we loved. And when any famous artist had died, we spent that night listening to and talking about their music...from Chris Cornell to Prince to Bowie. When we weren't talking about music, we were talking about life. We both had been English majors, so our likes and dislikes in literature were on the table...along with religion, politics, philosophy, travel, and our past relationships. We were never at a loss for words or topics, and we genuinely enjoyed and respected each other's minds. I had always maintained that we had logged more hours in deep conversation in less than a decade than most married people do in a lifetime. But this session was all about the deconstructing and processing of one of the darkest weekends of my life, followed up by the planning for the next day.

Needless to say, I'd have much preferred a trip to play pickleball and eat delicious treats at a pavilion in the park that Saturday over what had just transpired in the previous 28 hours. But there I was...unable to drive anywhere, facing a major surgery on my brain, and not knowing which critical thing to do next...as they all seemed critical at the time.

But the next immediate thought was, "Brennan, what if this mass is the cause of everything I've been experiencing for the past three years???"

2

Chapter 2: Drowning in (Mis)Diagnoses

(trigger warning)

July 2, 2018

It was meant to be a day of kayaking on the Brandywine with my friend of five short years and birthday-girl-pickleball-pro-peep, Lee. However, when I woke up on Monday morning, I faced an unwelcomed visitor. A stomach bug found its way to my microbiome and declared it a playground for the better part of three days. I thought I had eaten some bad eggs, and perhaps I had...because I had to use both the toilet and the trash can simultaneously for a full day, and I felt like a Mack truck had backed over me twice for the two days following that fun. In the days after those, I felt the slow but insistent creep of anxiety set in. Along with a craving for sugar and carbs. I had just finished a year of a hormone-balancing diet, on which I had lost 45 pounds and had avoided sugar and bad carbs (the simple ones)...so sugar/carb cravings were not something that I had been all that tempted by recently.

I was no stranger to anxiety, but I had not experienced it for many,

many years. However, anxiety was back *en force*, and she had brought a lot of baggage. She had apparently planned to stay for quite some time. Ben Franklin was right about fish and visitors...they both stink after three days. And anxiety was no exception.

On October 26, 2018, I woke up in a full-on panic. There was no immediate danger, but I had gone out to the sofa to try to rest better, as I had been restless and anxious all night long. The elephant who had been paying visits to my chest here and there for the past four months, was apparently tired. And she wasn't going anywhere. I went to work that day, full of fear for no real reason. I struggled through a field trip with our clients to the Princeton Museum. That evening, Brennan and I had dinner plans with good friends. As I faked smiles and little laughs throughout the meal, all I could think about was wanting to jump out of my skin...that I was so uncomfortable just being. And it got no better when Brennan and I went home.

"Brennan, this is awful," I cried out to him. He came over to the sofa and sat with me, stroking my hair as I laid my head on his lap.

"Why don't you just try to relax and go to sleep," he said as he put on some tunes.

And so I laid there, twitching uncontrollably, but trying super hard not to let Brennan feel my body shake. But it was no use, I could not relax. So I got up after a half hour, kissed him goodnight, and went to my bedroom. I changed into my pj's, crawled under the covers, and waited. I did some deep breathing techniques, but sleep just would not come. I tossed and turned and tossed some more. Eventually, I fell asleep for a few hours. But around 3 a.m., my body shook itself out of the light slumber it was in, and my mind began a series of back-to-back-to-back, long-distance sprints. The most random thoughts would appear from the deepest recesses of my memory...things like how I broke my friend's finger accidentally while playing field hockey in gym class in the seventh grade while my parents were away on a trip...and that my mother had saved all her tax returns from 1970 forward in the attic of our family home...and how my high school boyfriend decided I was too fat to keep dating after he put his hands around his ankles, calves, and biceps and then mine, only to prove that yes, indeed he was skinny, and I was not.

Unfortunately, this would be the first of 900 or so nights to come that followed the same pattern. As it turns out, when your brain doesn't get the rest it needs each night, it gets pretty angry during the day. I struggled to retain new information at work, but I tried my very best to hide my shortcomings, hoping that no one would notice. As anxiety decided to take full control of my every thought, feeling, waking moment, and every attempt-at-sleeping moment, she was front and center, demanding full attention 24/7. I could not imagine a worse existence. Because that was all I could do—exist.

Anxiety set up camp in a spare corner of my head, causing me to doubt my abilities to do the job I loved, not to be able to make decisions of any kind, and to worry about absolutely everything. I decided to go to my primary care physician; he wanted to start me on antidepressants. I told him that I had tried them all in my 20s, and that nothing had ever worked. He gave me some Xanax for the anxiety, which only worked for short periods of time. And eventually, I started on Klonopin. He also added Mirtazapine for depression. I eventually weaned myself off of these medicines because I had done what every doctor in the world hates—I googled the side effects and dangers. Addiction was a big one, and it caused me even more anxiety. Eventually, I weened myself off of these drugs and simply lived with the anxiety, which never went away, even when I was on the meds. And I just continued to get worse until the point I thought I'd lose my job.

One day in March of 2019, I had my weekly meeting with my boss. After going through the agenda items, he said to me, "Jordyn, I thought about you more than my own wife over the past week. What's going on?"

I had no response. He said what he did out of concern, but it only confirmed my worst fear…my job was in jeopardy. I wasn't fooling anyone. My insecurity, doubts, and fears were on full display for my colleagues and boss to see and pick apart.

June 2019

At the end of June 2019, I left a job that I loved in Princeton, NJ, in favor of one closer to my home with the hope that during the time I saved commuting to and from Princeton, I could find a medical practitioner who could figure out what was going on with me. But despite being a short, 10-minute commute, a new job didn't solve any problems. Rather, it only heightened my fears and doubts as I had to learn a whole new industry.

As the anxiety became more and more demanding on my body and mind, I began searching for some sort of holistic way to figure out and treat what was going on.

Enter a session with a reflexologist in August 2019, who in turn recommended a nearby certified nutrition coach. Of course, her services were not covered by insurance, as she was not a licensed medical practitioner, and her methods were, let's say "uncommon." For instance, in my first session, she "diagnosed" me with "most likely" Lyme disease. And she did this with the help of a funky, oversized "computer mouse" that sent electric currents, which I could not feel, all through my body when I placed my hand on it. This device was called a ZYTO scanner, believed by many to be bunk. These currents scanned my body and spat out a list on her computer of every virus, disease, infection, parasite, and basic intruder currently in my body.

The list was longer than my arm! What the ever-living &#$*? She convinced me to try a Lyme protocol for two months. AFTER I spent a month clearing my lymphatic system and treating possible parasites. While I was doing all this, I had to totally cut out all sugar, processed carbs, and stick to a quite minimal diet of mostly raw vegetables and platefuls of ice cubes. To say I was unhappy was nowhere near accurate...Mordor-pissed off was a touch closer to reality.

After three months of this living hell, I felt no better, and I decided to find a Lyme-literate functional medicine doctor in October of 2019. After going through all of my symptoms, she ran all the tests, most of which my new health insurance also did not cover, including the blood draw of 14 (!!!) vials of blood. She, too, determined I had Lyme disease and started me on a protocol of about 15 different homeopathic remedies and tinctures. When I mentioned some GI distress and pain, she recommended that I get a colonoscopy to rule out anything else in that realm.

So, on top of everything else I was worrying about, I had to get a colonoscopy to eliminate the possibilities of colon cancer, celiac disease, or IBS. Those weren't even on my radar. Thankfully, the test was a breeze, despite the awful magnesium concoction I had to drink that turned me into a veritable poop factory for the day leading up to the test. The upside to the colonoscopy was that I actually got decent sleep, if only for 20 minutes. It seemed like much longer, and that was all that mattered to me and my tired, tired mind.

"Good news," said Dr. Howell. "There were no polyps or areas of concern. I saw nothing to indicate anything but a healthy colon. You are good to go." Whew! That was exactly what I needed to hear. Well, that, and that someone could make me feel better. *Please, someone, anyone make this dreaded anxiety stop. Please!*

So, the following week, I went back to my functional medicine doctor. It was December 2019, and she started me on a four-month course of four different antibiotics to fight the Lyme Disease, plus the 15 other supplements. I hate taking antibiotics because of what they do to my gut, but I saw no other way. During a routine visit to my primary care doc, he took a look at my blood test results, with a funny and confused look on his face.

"So, she has you on a cocktail of four different antibiotics for Lyme Disease, right?" my doc asked me.

"Yes, that's right," I responded. I studied his face as he looked at the bloodwork results. "What's up, Doc?" Yeah...I couldn't resist that one.

"Well, I'm not a Lyme specialist, but according to this test," he continued, "you had Lyme at some point, but not now. This is a past infection showing antibodies...not a current infection."

"What?" I asked incredulously. "Seriously?"

"That's what I'm seeing here," said Dr. Frank.

I thanked Dr. Frank, and went on my way. At my next appointment, I asked Dr. Waters about whether my Lyme infection was a current one or a past one.

"Yes, of course it is current," she said.

"But then why is it showing up in this column instead of that one," I asked, trying to understand the difference between IgG and IgM, a Western blot test, and an ELISA test...all the while, none of it wanting to stick in my foggy gray matter. "My primary care physician says it looks like a past infection to him as well," I cautiously said to her.

"Look, Jordyn...blah, blah, blah, blah, blah," Dr. Waters went on with medicalese that I just did not get, and my anxiety was going through the roof as she spoke. "Just stay on the antibiotics for these few months. It should clear things up for you."

Reluctantly, I agreed, even though four antibiotics were the last things I wanted to be putting into my system. And yes, I was still on the no-sugar and highly modified diet. Weight fell off my frame for the first time in my life. As I became a shell of the person I was, I had no energy to do anything, but sleep still evaded me, unless of course I was trying to talk to Brennan at night. Then I would fall asleep mid-sentence somewhere between 7:30 and 8:00. But Brennan would let me sleep every night for as many minutes as I could before I would eventually wake up and put myself to bed around 9-ish. Only to lie awake for most of the night...or if I could get back to sleep for a tiny bit, I would wake again to body tremors from the anxiety. Hell would have been a desirable, permanent vacation spot compared to this daily routine.

Beyond my own physical and mental struggles, I felt like an awful partner to Brennan in every way imaginable.

"Brennan, this is not fair to you," I said, through a river of tears.

"Jordyn," he began. "Stop. I am fine. And I am here for you. We'll figure this out."

I decided to stop the antibiotics a bit short of the four months, as it just wreaked havoc on my system, and instead I opted for my homeopathic tinctures, vitamins, and the like. In early July, I had another complete blood work makeup done again to see if anything had changed.

Two Lyme bands went away on the Western Blot test, which made me very happy, except that I still felt like complete doo-doo all of the time. And Dr. Waters said I still had Lyme. I just wasn't getting any of this. And the anxiety was downright crippling by this point.

September 2020

After almost two full years of dealing with anxiety, and a year at a job that just didn't seem to fit me at all, I had had it.

So on September 14, 2020, I left a letter for Brennan on my bedroom dresser while he was out coaching youth soccer practice.

Brennan,

I wrote a page-long list of important things today...retirement logins, bank accounts and debit card pins, a few other random things...like where to find the title to my car. It's in my green ottoman with my Will.

There are no words to really describe how awful I feel most of the time. I can't think clearly at all...which affects everything I do. I can't make simple decisions. I struggle with small tasks. It shouldn't be this way, but it is. I'm virtually certain I'm going to lose my job...and because I lack so much knowledge (and the ability to learn them at the moment), I can't see myself getting another one. My meds will cost over $400/mo without insurance...and I don't want to throw away the money I've been saving. I want you to be able to get out of the apartment at the end of the lease by using the money in my bank account to pay the rent. So use the Bank of America app/login to move money to our joint account.

I don't see a way out of the bad decisions I've made in the last few years...and because of them, I'm suffering now. I don't want to suffer any longer...I just need peace.

You are my best friend, and I love you so much. I want you to be the best you possible...and maybe not drink so much. You were so good to me as I struggled...always encouraging me to keep fighting. But I won't be a drain on anyone...I can't do that. I wish the meds would have worked for me, but they didn't.

Know that I adore you and want you to be happy...I just couldn't get back to being happy myself. Make all your dreams come true and continue being a great dad, coach, and human being full of empathy. Remember our fun times, long talks, and trips together. And please remember me when I was happier.

I love you. Please tell my family I love them, too. I'm so sorry.

Then I changed clothes, putting on gym shorts, a sports bra, and a t-shirt, and I ran a warm bath around 7 p.m. I put a sticky note on the exterior side of the door to the apartment, telling Brennan not to come inside, but instead to go straight to the cops (who happened to be stationed right next door to us).

I got into the tub and shut off the water. Then I quickly learned just how hard it was to make all the air in my lungs leave so that water could take its place. Despite how things looked in the movies, drowning in a bathtub is actually hard for an adult. After several failed attempts, I got out, dried myself off, changed out of the shorts, sports bra, and t-shirt that I purposefully put on, so as not to be buck naked when the cops came to get me, and I put on other comfy, dry clothes.

I removed the sticky note from the front door, put the letter away, and just sat in the dark, living room quietly until Brennan got home around 8:30.

"Hey," he said as he opened the door. "Are you just sitting here in the dark?"

"Yep," I mustered, never looking at him...facing forward at a blank wall.

"OK," he said questioningly. "Is everything alright?"

I shrugged my shoulders and shook my head "no" ever so slightly.

"Guess what happened at practice tonight?" Brennan asked excitedly. Then the soccer talk ensued for an hour or so til I fell asleep to his talking...once again.

November 2020

In November of 2020, I decided to leave Dr. Waters behind in favor of a doctor in Arizona who specialized in EBV, which also showed up in my extensive blood work with Dr. Waters. EBV, also known as Epstein-Barr Virus, is commonly known as mononucleosis or Mono...yep, the kissing disease. Almost 90% of the world would test positive for EBV. If one has ever shared a drinking straw, eating utensil, or the like, chances are, they have the non-threatening form of EBV. This virus, like all viruses, stays in one's nervous system forever. The key is knowing when it is critical to address and treat, and when it's just hanging out there in the background like a wallflower at a party she really didn't want to go to.

One of the benefits of CRUD-19 is that doctors were open to treating people remotely...like not-even-in-the-same-state remotely. When I was recommended to Dr. Goodheart by another friend who had Lyme, she looked at my blood work, listened to my ever-growing tale of woe, and asked me to do yet another series of tests at my expense, as she, too, was a naturopathic doctor. Then she started me on a regime of inject-able treatments derived from a plant found in nature that was her own concoction.

Brennan was a trooper, giving me the shots in my posterior, two times each day. When that proved no help, I tried capsules, which were less bioavailable than the shots...but I was desperate for help. I gave all the EBV treatments the ol' college try, but inevitably, I let this go as well.

I was getting to the point of just accepting that I would have to live with debilitating anxiety forever. Because no one could seem to pinpoint what was going on, nor why it was going on.

And so, I soldiered on with no other choice than to just try to deal, try to sleep, try to think, try to be confident, try not to get fired, try.

Try.

Try.

Try again.

But always feeling like a complete and utter failure at every turn. Chronic anxiety is a thief's thief...winning the Blue Ribbon for destroying a person down to their very soul. It's lonely...bitterly, utterly lonely. But I loved Brennan for sticking by me for the previous two years, and I kept putting one foot in front of the other...for him. For my family in Texas and other parts of Pennsylvania. I could not do it for myself. I was a shell of my former self...physically, mentally, emotionally, spiritually. I did not recognize the woman standing in front of me when I looked in the mirror. In fact, I tried my best to avoid mirrors altogether.

I was in size 10 jeans and medium shirts by Spring 2021. I have never been that small in my life. Seriously...not even junior high. As much as I had dreamed of being thin every single day of my life, I did not want to get there this way...via anxiety. It was unhealthy weight loss. I was even more disgusted with my naked self than when I was 100 pounds heavier...so much sagging skin. The National Geographic boobs were the worst. Give it a minute...think about the naked pictures of women in National Geographic magazine. Yeah, that. I apologized over and over and over again to Brennan. Knowing I was gross to look at. Sweetly, he never saw it that way. At least he denied it if he did...and for that, I was thankful.

March 2021

In March of 2021, I began a bit more research into another Lyme-literate doc...and this one was a psychiatrist, which meant she could prescribe psychotropics. Maybe, just maybe, she could help my anxiety!

So I made an appointment with her, chatted about my symptoms, journey to get to her, and my blood work. Interestingly, she, like my primary care doc, also agreed that my Lyme infection was a past one. I couldn't decide if I should have been pissed off or grateful...given all the money I spent (summing about $10k out of pocket over the previous two years)...to have another Lyme specialist say "this is not a current Lyme thing you are dealing with."

"Ok, Dr. Miller," I began. "If it's not Lyme, and not EBV, what is causing my body and mind to go berserk every single day?"

"I'm not entirely sure, Jordyn," she said. "But I'm thinking it has to do with your age, and most likely menopause." Dr. Miller paused. "Menopause is an evil bitch for many, many a woman. You just might be one of those lucky ones she singles out for extra-special fun."

I giggled, because what else could I do...I mean, it was funny. And it would have been funnier if it weren't true.

"I do have to question, Dr. Miller...your idea of 'extra-special fun'," I quickly followed up. We both smiled and chuckled, because we knew this was no fun at all.

"I mean, listen...perhaps we need to go do Chinese toenail torture. Because at this stage, that looks appealing in comparison," I continued.

She knew I was kidding, but my point was definitely made and acknowledged. "Listen, Jordyn, I know you've tried a host of antidepressants and antipsychotics that did not work for you in the past," Dr. Miller said. "But if you are willing, I'd like you to try Duloxetine for a bit. It's a relatively newer drug, and you have not tried it before. Would you be willing to do that?"

What choice did I have? "Yes, I'll give it a shot," I said reluctantly. And so I left her office, script in hand, with only a smidgen of hope accompanying said script. *Here goes another big fat nothing,* I thought to myself.

But I picked up the script the next day and started on a small dose. I did my daily duty for a month, with just a touch of improvement. So Dr. Miller increased my dosage just a bit. I kept at it for two more months.

In the meantime, Brennan began doing some research on natural supplements from a brand that we had been taking proactively for a host of other issues we had hoped to prevent. Within a few days, Brennan came to me with emails from the owner of the company.

"Jordyn, look at this email," Brennan said. "It's from Brian Johnston.

I asked him if he had any products he'd recommend for a woman with your symptoms. He recommended one!" Brennan's enthusiasm was palpable. I think he wanted me to feel better as much or more than I did. "It's called Placenta."

"Interesting, Brennan," I said. "Super interesting. You told Brian I never had kids, right? And that I don't have all my female parts anymore...yes?"

"Yeah, Jordyn...he knows. And it's part of the reason he recommends the Placenta supplement."

"Ummmm...OK. Let's give it a go," I conceded to the pricey supplement. I mean, after spending more than $10k, what was another $70?

"Great!" Brennan exclaimed. "I just ordered it. Should be here in two days."

"Thank you," I said, with the tiniest sliver of hope in my voice.

Two days later I began my daily regimen of Placenta capsules. Unbelievably, on Day 3, I began to feel just the slightest bit better. I mean, it wasn't a silver bullet or anything, but my goodness, I felt like not dying for the first time in 2.5 years! I almost could not believe it! I had found something that made a truly noticeable, albeit slight, difference. And at this point, I would take a "difference" over chronic anxiety. By Day 7, I was actually sleeping a teensy bit better! Anxiety was still hanging out in my attic. Kicking her feet up on my gray matter every hour or so, just to let me know she wasn't going anywhere, despite what this new interloper might be doing in an attempt to get her to leave.

Brennan and I were both thrilled with the Placenta results. So I kept going with them, and I told Dr. Miller about them. She was happy that something was helping me, even if it was only marginally. I also told her I wanted to cut back on the duloxetine. She agreed I could cut back to see what happened. Eventually, I stopped them altogether by the time summer rolled around.

3

Chapter 3: Consults, Customer Service, and Complete Confidence

September 28, 2021

The day had arrived...three consultations with three different, highly rated neurosurgeons in the two most prestigious hospitals in Philadelphia, which coincidentally were also two of the top three hospitals in the entire state of Pennsylvania. Brennan took me to my appointment at the Hospital of the University of Pennsylvania, where I first met with Dr. A. He had just left his position at UPMC in Pittsburgh, which coincidentally was the #2 ranked hospital in PA, and began his role as Neurosurgeon and Director of the Penn Brain Tumor Center. His Physician Assistant, Elizabeth, met with me first. She was sweet, lovely, and a pro. She let me know what to expect in terms of paperwork, pre-op, and a bit about Dr. A., should I decide to have my surgery at Penn.

When Elizabeth had finished, I sat in the office alone, waiting for Dr. A. Within a few minutes, a tall, distinguished-and-smart-looking, bespectacled man in a lab coat walked in and sat down on the other side of the desk from me.

"Hi, Jordyn! I am Dr. A.," the impressive man said to me, with a kind softness I wasn't really prepared for. "We've received your scans from your hospital stay earlier this month. How are you feeling today?"

I took a deep breath in and began, "Well, I've got a lot going on, or so they tell me. And I have screaming anxiety 24/7. Is there any chance this tumor and my anxiety are connected?"

He smiled, nodded his head, and began. "Yes, there is a definite connection," said Dr. A. He pulled up my MRI onto the monitor in front of him and turned the screen so we both could see it as he spoke "You see this spot here in your right temporal lobe?" He proceeded to air-circle with his lidded pen. "That is your meningioma, and it's about the size of a quarter."

I shook my head incredulously. "What?" I asked. "Something that small is causing so much upheaval in my head, body, and life? Really?"

"Yes, unfortunately it is," said Dr. A. "And you're going to feel so much better once it comes out."

Having worked for an early-onset dementia organization ten years prior to this, I knew a little bit about the areas of the brain and what each one does. So I asked, "Wait...if the tumor sits in the temporal lobe, why is it the cause of my anxiety? It's not in the amygdala where flight and fight lives."

"Well, Jordyn, the brain is a strange, strange thing, and it doesn't always behave the way we think it will," Dr. A. quickly answered. "Let me assure you...you are going to feel so much better after we remove this." Then he went on to explain the procedure and how it was a routine surgery. I sat there thinking, *Yeah, brain surgery...routine. Sure.* But he oozed a quiet, calm confidence that was simultaneously disarming **and** comforting.

"How soon would you want to do the surgery?" I asked him.

"Well, this is not a life-threatening thing, so you don't have to have it done immediately. But I am still pretty new here, I just began at the beginning of this month, so my surgery calendar is pretty light at this point. So..." he pulled up a calendar on the monitor. "I could do the surgery two Fridays from now...on October 8. Then you'll be rid of this thing and can get on with your life."

"Well, that certainly sounds good," I said. "The sooner, the better." Then another question popped into my anxious mind. "Oh, may I ask what made you want to become a neurosurgeon?"

Dr. A. paused for just a second, then said, "Well, my father passed away from brain cancer, so my work is very, very personal."

I paused for a moment to acknowledge his connection to his work. "I see," I finally said. "I am sorry for your loss." He thanked me, and gave me an approving nod to continue.

My next question was about aphasia...because I also worked for a tech company that made speech-generating devices for people who have had a stroke and then had trouble with their speech and communication. So I had to ask the question...

"Tell me, is there any chance that I might wake up from surgery with aphasia?"

Taking no time at all to answer, Dr. A. said, "No, none."

I nodded in acceptance, saying "I just want to have my former boss on call with a speech-generating device already programmed for me, should I need one."

"Don't worry, Jordyn. I got you," said Dr. A. And with that, he asked, "Hey, do you have your cell phone handy?"

"Yes," I said, reaching into my purse.

"Great, type in this number," he said, as he recited the ten digits that would ring and text his cell phone. "If you have any questions about the procedure, the post-op, or anything at all, please call or text me." I dutifully, yet dumbfoundedly, put the number into my phone under "Dr. A., Penn."

"I do have one question now," I said. "If you do the surgery on a Friday, will you be around over the weekend to check in on me?"

Dr. A. chuckled just a bit, but quickly replied, "Jordyn, I'm not going anywhere until you go home from the hospital."

I quietly paused for a moment to take in what had just happened. A Yale-educated, world-class neurosurgeon just gave me his cell phone number. What doctor of any kind gives out his cell number...let alone a neurosurgeon who just met me? I had not even agreed to have him do the surgery yet...but he just gave me his cell number. And he was going to be around to check on me after the surgery, even on a weekend.

I had two other consultations with other neurosurgeons set up for later that day, but something in my gut told me he was going to be my doctor.

"Do you have any other questions right now?" Dr. A. asked.

I shook my head, saying "No, I think I'm good for now."

"Great, Elizabeth will walk you out. It was a pleasure to meet you, and don't forget to call or text me with any other questions that come up."

"Thank you, Dr. A., I will," I said, and with that, he left the office. Elizabeth returned in a few minutes, walked me out to Billing, and said her goodbyes to me as well.

I had an hour to spare before my consult at the other hospital. So I went down to the car where Brennan waited to take me to the next appointment, filled him in on what I had learned upstairs, and then we headed to the next doctor interview. When I finally made it to the right department, I met with Dr. Smith. He gave me many of the same answers to my questions as Dr. A.

"Yes, this is a common procedure, pretty straightforward, I've done hundreds of these," he said. But then I asked if he would be around over the weekend to check on me. "Well, if I am on call, I will be here. Otherwise, another colleague will attend to you."

I sat back in my chair. In my mind, this was not the right answer. I wanted the answer that Dr. A. gave me. I did not get it. And with that, I decided to cancel the third consult, and left the hospital.

I debriefed all of this with Brennan on the way home. I knew I had my neurosurgeon...Dr. A. was the one.

I took the night to sleep on it, and in the morning, I sent Dr. A. a text message:

> Me: Hi Dr. A. This is Jordyn Osborne. We met yesterday regarding my meningioma. I would like for you to do my surgery next Friday at noon. I've sent

a confirmation email to Elizabeth, and
I will be in on Thursday to do my
pre-op exams at 11 am. Thank you for
your time yesterday, I can't wait to be
tumor-free!

An hour and a half later, Dr. A. texted me back.

Dr. A.: Hi Jordyn! I'm so happy to hear
this. You know we will take good care of
you. And I can't wait for you to be
tumor-free!!

And just like that, my brain tumor surgery was in the books...scheduled for three weeks to the day after the seizure in my kitchen.

I spent the next few days getting my mind right and prepared for brain surgery...not that there's a book or manual you can read for such a thing. But I knew I needed to try to be in the best frame of mind as possible. That included sitting down with Brennan and my mom the day before my surgery to go over a few things.

We gathered at our dining room table, Brennan to my left, Mom to my right, and I sat at one end of the table. I had a manilla folder with papers and blue ink in my handwriting all over them. I began.

"OK, so...in the event that things do not go as planned, I want both of you to know where all of my important documents are, my logins, my passwords, and who gets what according to my will."

They both sat back, took out their own pieces of paper and pens, and we went through it all.

"OK, here is a list of all my logins and passwords for email accounts, bank accounts, credit card accounts, and more. I have three bank accounts...each of you, plus Stacy is a beneficiary for one. I have two IRAs, and Brennan is beneficiary for this one...Mom and Stace will split the other. The information for my car loan is here."

I shuffled a few sheets around and continued. "This is my Will. My lawyer's name and location are here," I said, pointing to my handwritten sheet. "Brennan will get all of my stuff, because, well, Mom...you and Stace already have your own stuff. Brennan needs my stuff more than you do." Mom seemed to understand that, and nodded in agreement. "Oh, and there is a small account that should be used for my cremation. That way it doesn't come out of the accounts designated for you."

I took one more breath, looked at both of them, and said, "I do not want to be resuscitated if I am simply going to be a vegetable. So there is a DNR clause in my will." They nodded in acknowledgment and understanding. "That's it. Any questions?"

"No, I think I've got it," said Brennan. "I took good notes."

"I'm good, too," said Mom. "But we are not going to need any of this, Jordyn."

I understood that my mother did not want to entertain the worst-case scenario, but in reality, none of us ever does. It's like the lyrics of my second-favorite Rival Sons song:

> *Nobody wants to die, but they know they're gonna have to*
> *Silver and gold, people you know*
> *Ain't nothin' gonna save you.*

4

Chapter 4: Evacuation Day

October 8, 2021

Time to remove the unwanted guest from my brain. In another strange twist of events, I actually slept well last night. Maybe it was the tryptophan in the turkey I had for dinner, maybe it was just the tiredness from the week catching up with me, or maybe it was the amazing support that so many had given me during the week. I chose to believe it was the latter...and was so very grateful for it.

My mom stayed with us the night before, and my sister flew up from Houston to be here for the surgery. They were staying in downtown Philly at a hotel for the next few days, as our apartment would not accommodate everyone.

I had planned to work the morning of my surgery, as my scheduled surgery time was around 5 p.m. I wasn't thrilled about such a late-day operation for a few reasons...not being able to eat all day long, having to think about the upcoming surgery all day long, and perhaps the most important one: Dr. A. would have other surgeries ahead of me. I was really hoping for an early morning procedure, so he would be fresh!

As I sat at the dining room table, I worked on a few items for my job.

But around 9:05 a.m., my phone rang. It was someone from Penn. They wanted to know if we were on our way yet.

"Ummmm...no, I am not scheduled for surgery until 5 p.m. We weren't planning to leave until around 2 p.m."

The voice at the other end of the phone replied, "Dr. A. had a cancellation, so we need you to come in now. Your surgery has been moved up to noon."

"Oh, ummmm, ok. We will get ready and come in as soon as we can! But I need to finish packing my toiletries. We'll do our best."

This was not what I needed...I had my day mapped out in my mind, and a last-minute change involving getting in the car STAT was not part of it. However, the silver linings were that Dr. A. would be super-fresh, I wouldn't have to be awake for as long with no food, and this would all be over sooner than later.

I got Brennan and Mom in gear, grabbed my last few items from the bathroom, slung my hospital bag–which had been packed for days–over my shoulder, grabbed my folder of surgery info, and we headed down to my car.

As Brennan drove downtown, I received another call from the hospital.

The voice at the other end said, "Hello, we were wondering if you are coming in for your surgery today. You should be here by now."

Half-panicked, half-annoyed, I responded, "Yes, we are on our way! But you should know that I only found out about the schedule change 45 minutes ago...this was not my fault." I glanced down at Waze to see how much longer it would be until we arrived at the hospital. "We will be there in 15 minutes."

"Ok, great. We'll see you when you get here," said the scheduler.

Fifteen minutes later, Brennan dropped Mom and me off at the hospital entrance while he parked a few blocks away in the hospital garage. I checked in at the nurses' station, and Mom and I sat down. While we waited for Brennan, I asked Mom to get out her phone.

"Hey Mom, I know you probably don't listen to a lot of music on your phone, but can you download Spotify? It's free."

As she did that, I pulled up my playlists, and located the one called "Mom 10.08.21"

"OK, I've got it," she said.

"Great. Now, I'm going to share a playlist that I made for you for today," I said. "I figured you could use something to keep you busy while you wait for surgery to be finished. So here are some of the songs we used to listen to in the mountains—when Stace and I were young—some of your favorites. I put on some Bee Gees, some old school country music, and just some songs that had great lyrics. Songs like 'Don't You Worry 'Bout a Thing,' 'Stacy's Mom,' and 'Shower the People.'

"Oh my goodness, Jordi!" Mom exclaimed. "How long did it take you...you had so much..." her voice trailed off as she looked over the playlist. "Michael McDonald, Elvis, Alabama, Third Day."

"Yes, they are all there," I smiled. Then my sister walked in. She had just been dropped off by her Uber from her hotel in Center City. We hugged and sat back down after she got her visitor's badge and signed in.

"Hi!" she said. "How's everybody doing this morning? Are we ready to do this?" she asked exuberantly.

"Yep, all set. Just waiting for them to come get me," I replied. "Hey, I have something for you...get out your phone." I waited a minute, then said, "OK, open your Spotify." She did so, and then I shared my Stacy playlist with her. It contained some silly songs with special meaning to both of us, like a Rusted Root song, "S.O.B." by Nathaniel Rateliff & the Night Sweats, some Dave Matthews Band songs (Stacy chased down his tour bus once when she was in college), and of course, "What's Up?" by 4 Non Blondes. Stacy "sang" that song at the top of her lungs on a trip to North Carolina with my college friends in the car. And she would always get the words to songs wrong when she sang them...cracked both of us up.

"Wow, Jord...this is awesome! Thank you. I can't believe you..." her voice stopped as she looked over her playlist as well.

Brennan was back from parking. He signed in, hugged Stacy, and sat down. His turn. I gave everyone a handwritten card, gave a Sudoku book to my mom as an extra distraction, and proceeded to give Brennan his playlist. Despite being a huge music fan, Brennan did not have Spotify on his phone. For some reason, he had just resisted...saying he had the music he wanted already saved to his phone. Whatever. I told him in his card that he should just "download the freakin' app and listen to the playlist." He thanked me, and a minute later, they called me to go upstairs to be admitted and prepped for surgery. Only two guests could go with me at a time...surgery in the age of CRUD-19. So the three of them talked, and they decided that Mom would stay downstairs for the time being, so Brennan and Stacy went with me for prep.

Eventually, I was all set. Blind as a bat, because, well...no glasses. But I was in today's version of Dress Blues with the opening in the back. My bladder, like the rest of me, was 48 years old and wanted to "take some off the top" much more often than I preferred. So I was up and down, back and forth with an IV drip hanging off my arm as I went to and from the bathroom. The other hand tried to hold the back of my gown closed tight, so as not to pull a Jack Nicholson in *Something's Gotta Give*. No need to recreate my version of the "Dancing Henries" before surgery.

Stacy hugged me, wished me well, and told me she loved me. I gave her my phone, showed her the two text groups I had set up for her to message with updates–one close friend group, and one family group. She had already created a Facebook thread telling hundreds of people about my surgery and asked for thoughts, prayers, and good vibes today. Then Stacy traded spots with Mom downstairs, so she could come see me before I went into the OR. Mom kissed me, hugged me, and told me she loved me. Brennan was the last to go. He kissed me and wished me well. I told him I loved him, and that was that. Off I went. I was ready...ready to be "Jordyn Version 2.0," as I would commonly refer to myself in the blog that I started just after my seizure to process all that was happening. And the best part of Jordyn 2.0 was that this version was going to be delivered bug-free!

The surgery went just according to plan. Dr. A. successfully removed my entire meningioma, which sat just north of my right ear, by cutting out a piece of my skull, then resecting the mass. Easy peasy...no mass, no *mas*!

After Dr. A. put me back together, he spoke to Mom, Stace, and Brennan; and then everyone went home for the night–Dr. A. to his home in Philly, Mom and Stace to the hotel in Center City, and Brennan back to our apartment in the 'burbs. I was wheeled to the ICU, but I have no recollection of anything...I was still happily in la-la land.

# # # # #

Just as Brennan was pulling into the parking lot at our complex around 9 p.m., his phone rang. A doctor, who seemed to be running down a corridor, was on the other end of the call.

"Is this Brennan?" the doctor asked.

"Yes, it is," Brennan said with some trepidation upon seeing an unknown Philadelphia number show up with the incoming call.

"Brennan, I am Dr. Love at the Hospital of the University of Pennsylvania. You are listed as one of Jordyn's emergency contacts," he said. "She is going back into emergency surgery right now. Her care team in the ICU saw some suspicious stuff during rounds."

"Ummmm, what does that mean, Dr. Love? What is suspicious stuff?" asked Brennan.

"She has a bleed on the brain," Dr. Love quickly replied. "We'll be back in touch as soon as we know more."

"F&%$. Ok, thanks for the call," said Brennan, not believing his ears. He hung up with Dr. Love and immediately called Stacy to tell her the news.

Stacy went into high-alert mode: Time to call in the cavalry...time to call on Calvary. Text messages were sent out to the family and friends text groups on my cell, a message was posted on her Facebook page, tagging me so that all of my contacts and friends would know it was time to pray...and pray hard, fast, and often. And with that, people from all over the country—people whom I had never met, people who did not know me from Eve, and people who loved me like their own family—stopped whatever they were doing to send out pleas for my life to be spared. Her next text was to Dr. A.

Stacy: Dr. A., This is Stacy, Jordyn's sister. I imagine you already know this, but the hospital called Brennan around 9 p.m., saying Jordyn developed a blood clot and they were rushing her in to try to save her. How can we get updates on her status? As you can imagine we are all going crazy and very scared. Is there a number we can call to check in on her?

Within minutes, a reply came back.

Hospital Staffer: Dr. A. is in the OR now. This is the circulator. She had some unexpected bleeding, but everything is under control now.

Stacy took a deep breath, told Mom, called Brennan, and sent out another round of updates via text and Facebook...thanking everyone for their prayers. My people took a collective breath of relief and tried to settle back into their sleep and chill time after a long day that took a scary turn, but recovered thanks to a skilled care team and awesome neurosurgeon.

Lo and behold...the pleas from my tribe who interceded on my behalf were heard by a merciful God, Spirit, Universe, and likely a host of other names invoked from a multitude of places across the country. Dr. A. stopped the bleed to an artery that the meningioma had compressed while taking up its residency. Crisis averted—he stopped the bleed, put the piece of skull back into place, and stitched up my scalp. He cleaned up from the blood bath he had just taken courtesy of my angry artery, took a few breaths, and found a place to lie down for the night. He was beat, but he decided it best to stay at the hospital that night...just in case. No sense in having to rush back in again in the event of the unthinkable.

5

∿

Chapter 5: Well, That Didn't Go As Planned

October 9, 2021

Just after midnight the morning after my surgery, the attending staff tried to wake me from the anesthesia used during my emergency surgery. Apparently, that was not something the twice-agitated artery felt like enduring...and it made sure everyone knew. My pupils went berserk again, and Dr. A. was summoned back into the OR for his third surgery on me in less than 10 hours.

And with that, more Facebook requests went out for prayers, thoughts, vibrations, and anything else that could be mustered.

Dr. A. stepped back into his theater—new scrubs, new gloves, new tools, same patient, same problem, same attack plan—stop this bleed and save my life. Again. He sent out his own silent prayer this time for the life that rested in his hands, at this new-to-him hospital, with a new-to-him team, under circumstances with 1-in-10,000 odds of happening. Dr. A. did what he was trained to do. He stopped a second bleed, saved my life a second time, and breathed his own sigh of relief as he stitched me up. But he was not terribly hopeful or convinced that his work was over. He chose not to put the piece of skull back in its place. To his thinking, the artery wall had been eroded by 5-7 years, maybe up to 20 years, of compression by a meningioma. Once the tumor had been removed, blood was then free to flow fast and furiously through it. And the wall was just so weak in that spot.

After a time of recovery and clean up on his part, he sat down to rest. He knew he needed to rest because he did not know what might lay ahead of him in another few hours. He called Stacy at 3:30 a.m. to update her.

"Jordyn is out of surgery and in recovery. I am still here and not going anywhere. We're keeping her heavily sedated and keeping her intubated. We're also giving her steroids to keep the swelling down."

A nurse was stationed in my room to constantly monitor me. Shortly after 11 a.m. on Saturday, they wheeled a mobile CT scanner into my room so as not to make any sudden movements with me, literally. At almost 1 p.m. the results came back, showing no additional bleeds, but they wanted to keep me fully sedated in an effort to keep things calm. An MRI was ordered for later in the day, and it, too, showed no additional bleeds.

For the remainder of Saturday and into Sunday, all was quiet on the temporal lobe front. Brennan sat with me for most of Sunday. I began to make some progress on Sunday, moving my left shoulder and toes on both feet. I really hated that intubation tube and tried to yank it out a bunch, until they strapped my arms to the gurney. Apparently, I had some fight in me...probably from my feisty grandma. They gave me some more sedatives to help me relax and not fight the tube so much.

My sister texted Dr. A. when I started to move my left side due to her prompting. He called Stacy back immediately, asking "Are you sure it's her left side that's moving?"

"Ummm, yeah, it's her left side," Stacy snickered slightly, thinking to herself, *'I do know my left from my right.'* Dr. A. was shocked by that news. At 3:45 p.m. on Sunday, Mom, Stacy, and Brennan met with Dr. A. to discuss all that transpired and what everyone could expect.

"So, I did not put the piece of skull back into place yesterday because although she made it through the second breakthrough bleed, I thought that I was going to operate on her until she died or bled out," Dr. A. said with as much candor and comfort as he could manage. "But here we are...all is well and she's moving her left side, which is more than I ever hoped for," he paused for a moment. "So what comes next is some rehab. When she is ready, we'll do about a week or so of in-patient rehab to get her walking with a walker, bathing herself, generally, doing everything she needs to do to care for herself. Then later, I'll get a composite piece made to replace the missing piece of her skull. That will be a quick and easy procedure. But first things, first." He paused again. "She is one lucky woman...she is my miracle baby."

I spent the next three days in ICU, before they moved me to a step-down room, and then eventually to in-patient rehab not far from Penn. I do not remember any of these days, nor what took place during them. My earliest recollection was at in-patient rehab, a full week after my initial surgery. I have dubbed those first seven days *my Fentanyl brain days.* They were designed so that I didn't remember what happened to me, and it worked.

On October 14, I texted Dr. A.

> Me: Thank you for saving my life.
> –Jordyn

For the first time in three years, I felt ZERO anxiety. Despite the tales I was hearing about what I just survived, I felt completely calm, at ease, and dare I say, happy! My goodness, Dr. A. was right about the anxiety being gone as well. I just couldn't believe my luck. But I knew it was more than luck...it was thousands of prayers, good vibes, and well wishes from every corner of the country on my behalf.

Less than an hour later, he replied.

> Dr. A.: You are a special human being.
> You had me really worried, but we
> pulled through together!"

Over the next week, I texted him sporadically as I did my in-patient therapy to get stronger, to walk with a walker, to shower with help and then by myself, to play ping pong. And yes, I was better than everyone else...and none of them had brain surgery the week and half prior. Guess my athleticism was still intact.

On October 17, I texted him regarding my concerns about the next surgery I would have to have in December to replace the missing piece of my skull. I asked if we could talk about it, as I was not excited at all about having yet another surgery, as my stomach was not responding well to some of the meds and drinking thickened liquids was a torture from the devil himself...so gross.Dr. A. responded, saying that the skull reconstruction would be just cosmetic, would take 30 minutes to complete, and that it was what he had to do to save my life. He assured me the hard part was over, and I would be back to my old self before I knew it.

Me: I wasn't expecting it to be quite like this...I mean, I'm totally happy to be alive, but I'm just concerned about being intubated again.

Dr. A.: I know! It could have been fatal. This was a 1/10,000 event. And you are lucky. I know it doesn't seem that way, but, boy am I glad you had your surgery in a place where we have 24-hour supervision and that I live less than 10 minutes from the hospital. Someone was looking out for you!

Actually, a whole tribe of people were looking out for me. One of them made a trip from Charleston, SC to pay me a visit and bring a special dinner request to offset the yucky food in rehab. Katy had always been my "go-the-extra-mile" friend, and she was at it again. Flying north to pay me a visit in rehab while stopping in to see her dad in Lancaster as well. Holly also took time out of her schedule to bring flowers and cheer, and Lee and Shelagh helped to drive Mom to and from rehab when Brennan had to be at his computer for work. Not to mention the many texts and calls from family and friends far and wide.

During one of our text conversations, Dr. A. told me,

Dr. A.: In the grand scheme of my life
events, the ones that have made the
biggest impact on his life were my
wedding, the birth of his children,
and the moment that I learned
that Jordyn Osborne could move
her left side. Neurology and
neurosurgery are so very humbling...
and for reasons just like your
situation...weird stuff
happens that you can't predict.

He is an amazing doctor, and I'm eternally grateful to him and for him. And what's more, I believed him when he said how happy he was to learn that I could use my left side. No one saw any of this coming or even as a possibility, but it happened, and now, we had to deal with some therapy/recovering, and one more "cosmetic but important" surgery to put in a protective piece on my skull to cover my brain a bit in case of a fall/bump/accident. He said it should be a 20-minute procedure, and that I could do it without being intubated...YA-HOOOOOO!!!!

6

Chapter 6: Kindness, Compassion, and Brain Surgery Be Damned

December 2021 - November 2012
and back to December 2021 again

I went back to work part time in December. There were only a few times that I had to go into the office, and Brennan would drive me to and from when that happened. Otherwise, I worked from home. My second planned surgery took place on December 10. I asked my mom and sister not to come back for this one...I figured if I didn't make a big deal about it, it wouldn't be a big deal. So Brennan took me in for my new "skull helmet" as it was called.

I'd be lying if I said that I wasn't scared, given what happened the last time I had surgery on my head. But I tried to focus on the facts...and the facts were these: Dr. A. was not removing an invader this time, he was putting in a covering over a hole so that my brain was protected against falls and such, and it was a short surgery that Dr. A. made it seem like he could do this with his eyes closed...but he promised he wouldn't. The composite piece would be attached with titanium screws, and thankfully, they would not set off any metal detectors at airports. That was kind of a big deal to me, as a person with massive wanderlust.

As it turns out, Dr. A. was spot on...it was a short procedure with no complications and no intubation necessary. I was released the next day and started back to work part-time that Monday. Brennan and I had a vacation planned to Florida to visit his parents starting on Christmas Day, so I figured I would just do partial days until after the new year, then go back full time.

Brennan's 18-year-old son was a freshman at a university in Philadelphia, and he left school for winter break on December 16. Clay spent most of his time with his mother, Lorelei, and new stepfather, James.

Lorelei divorced Brennan about nine years prior, and it was one of the ugliest partings I had ever witnessed. Brennan didn't put up a fight at all, he had just wanted peace...but that was not to be. Lorelei made sure that she lived up to her namesake. There weren't many that refused her siren call. Poor Brennan just couldn't bear the thought of not seeing Clay each day, so he put up with her multitudinous transgressions against their marriage bed, her garnering of his paychecks while she lived a Desperate Housewives life of leisure, and her controlling...controlling which friends he saw, his smoking, and his drinking. So, when Brennan and I became good friends after Lorelei had kicked him out, she began stalking his every move, his every phone call and text message recipient via the phone bill. She even called my number, since it showed up on the bill. She left a voicemail demanding that I call her. I never did, and Brennan apologized over and over again for her intrusion. When it came to divorce proceedings, Lorelei got a good lawyer who went after Brennan's 401k and extorted him for $1,000/month for child support...far more than any court system would have demanded. Then Lorelei sold the house that Brennan signed over to her so that Clay could stay in the same place and school district. She kept every single cent from that sale and then moved Clay to a new school district anyway.

\# \# \# \# \#

I had met Brennan a little over a year before either of us went through our divorces. We ended up on the same volleyball team at a local Y. I had asked the league coordinator if he could put me on any team that needed a female player, and that particular season, Brennan's team needed a female for the co-ed roster. We would chat occasionally, like I did with all my teammates. And when I left my marriage, I needed to move into a new place. The one major problem was that I had no muscle to do the heavy lifting. Three of my girlfriends were up to the task, but I knew I would need some testosterone for this job. So I emailed the three men on my team with whom I spoke most often, but only Brennan was available to help.

After my friends and I had moved all the boxes from the UHaul into my new apartment, we enjoyed a hamburger BBQ lunch that my mom made, hung out for a bit, and then everyone headed out late in the afternoon...except for Brennan. He knew that the cable guy was supposed to show up, and he didn't want me to be in a new place by myself with a stranger. However, the cable guy was going to be late, a lot late. But Brennan didn't budge. It was well past 6:30 p.m. until the cable guy was finished doing his thing, and Brennan decided it was OK to leave after that. So around 7:00 or so, we said goodbye, and I gave him a card, like I had my girlfriends. I had put a gift card in everyone's card, because moving anyone stinks. And Brennan's was a little extra, since he did the super hard work. I figured he could use the extra as well, since he was sleeping on a friend's couch after his wife kicked him out of the house he paid for.

Brennan's job was literally 30 seconds from my new place. And so over the course of the next year and a few months, Brennan would come hang out after work at my place. We would sit in the same spots each night that he didn't have his son. His was right inside my door in an armless chair, and mine was the love seat across the room, which was conveniently close to the iPod player. We both loved music, and we listened to tunes every single night, talking about our favorite bands, concerts, and so much more. We were both English majors, so literature was always a topic we could draw upon, but finding something to talk about was never an issue. Despite never having visited Blarney Castle nor Ireland, this man with Eire in his blood most certainly had the gift of gab. We would occasionally go out for beverages, a local hike, or to shoot pool, and we couldn't pass up a local music fest with headliners Alice in Chains and Soundgarden. We became fast friends who enjoyed each other's company at a time when both of us could use a friend who understood the other's situation.

# # # # #

A year later when Brennan and I decided to share expenses and become roommates, Lorelei really dug her heels in. Despite all outward appearances (not the least of which was a divorce that had been final for 16 months) that she didn't want Brennan anymore, she clearly did not want anyone else to have him either, but it was too late for that. I was in love with my best friend, albeit a battered, bruised, and broke(n) best friend. Enter the first night that Brennan had Clay over to our apartment, when Clay was just 11 years old. I wanted to give them some privacy, but I also wanted to make Clay feel welcome. So I put on my hospitality hat and made him a batch of Rice Krispie treats with chocolate chips in them, then I made myself scarce. Apparently, Clay loved these treats so much that he went home and told his mother all about them. The next thing I knew, Brennan received a nasty call from Lorelei about the treats. Something along the lines of "What does she think she's doing? Trying to make me look bad? You need to do something about this, Brennan!"

The next day, she mentioned my crime against humanity to her girl-friends, who quite rightly and quickly said something to the effect of, "Lorelei, she could have been awful to Clay…but she wasn't. She treated him nicely. Shouldn't you be happy about that?"

Truth. While the truth was something Lorelei wasn't super familiar with, she couldn't deny that one, and she actually told Brennan about it. And apparently "thanked me for being nice to Clay" via Brennan.

Then came soccer. Brennan coached Clay's soccer team, and I wanted to be supportive of both of them. And as it happened, I ended up at more games than Lorelei...she was just *so* busy. So early on, when we were both at a game, she took the opportunity to begin poisoning Clay where I was concerned.

"Clay, did you see the way she was looking at me today at the soccer game? She was giving me dirty looks," Lorelei began planting the seeds of disdain for me in her young son's mind. Nevermind the fact that I had sunglasses on during said game...nice try, though, Lorelei. But the young boy didn't know how, when, or why to question his mother's judgment. He simply went along with it...after all, she was his mother. And she did a bang-up job of grooming him to dislike every kindness I ever showed to him, to not say thank you to me, and ignore me. She did it in subtle ways, as well as overt ways.

After every weekend Clay had been with us, he would be grilled by his mother with the same line of questioning: 1. "What did you do this weekend?" 2. "Was it just you and Dad?" 3. "Did Jordyn go along?" And by chance, if I did go along to a movie or family meal with Brennan's parents/sister, the questions were then turned on Brennan...as if he had no right to invite me to such things.

This kind of thing continued for the next seven years, until Clay was just straight up rude, disrespectful, and out of line when he visited our place. He almost never said hello or goodbye to me when entering or leaving our place, and rarely spoke to me unless he wanted something from me. He almost never thanked me for the food I bought when we went out to eat (Brennan couldn't afford it with a $1,000/month support payment), the Christmas and birthday gifts I would buy him, nor the soccer games that I would come to watch him play. He resented me, just like his mother resented me. And after years of his disrespect for no good reason, I grew to resent Clay, too. Brennan could have corrected his behavior, but no. Clay was allowed to do and say whatever he pleased. Brennan said he was giving Clay room to "express himself."

So, when winter break of his freshman year at college rolled around, Clay was supposed to spend December 20-24 at our place. Since we were leaving for Florida on Christmas morning to see Brennan's parents,

Brennan wanted to see Clay before we left. This all sounded just fine, until Clay let it slip that he was going to a big rap concert on Temple's campus the night of the 20th.

This was at the height of the COVID Omicron outbreak, and I was stunned that Brennan was going to allow Clay to go to the show. I mean, Brennan and I had strict rules that we abided by regarding COVID. We didn't go anywhere except to the grocery store, the liquor store, and occasionally, I went into a fairly dead office. That was it. And we wore our masks religiously.

It took me all of 30 seconds to figure out what was going to happen at this superspreader event: teenage college students were going to be jam packed in a mosh pit, masks were going to come off, and plenty of germs were going to be spread around like cow manure in Lancaster County. And then Clay was going to come back to our place? I had just survived brain surgery twice, almost died twice, and now I was supposed to gracefully accept the real possibility of having to endure COVID-19 on top of all this? I was incredulous.

I confronted Brennan about this the day before the concert. His response was also incredulous. "Jordyn, what do you want me to do? The tickets were an early Christmas gift from Lorelei."

I bit my tongue hard, this time willingly and on purpose, because what I wanted to say was, *"I don't care if they are from the Royal Queen of England!"* (God rest her soul.)

What I said instead was, "How much were the tickets? Maybe $100? I'll pay him $200 NOT to go. I don't want him bringing COVID back to this apartment...only for us to test positive and have to waste the $900 we each spent on tickets to Florida, or to turn around and give it to your folks! Have you thought about what your sister will say if that happens?"

"Yeah, that did cross my mind," admitted Brennan. "Listen, I'll talk to Lorelei about this. Maybe Clay and his friends can just go back to her beach house in Jersey after the concert."

"Also, are you really telling me that you are OK with my having to endure COVID after brain surgery...all because your son wants to see a rap concert?" I added in for good measure.

That comment was promptly ignored, and I walked away from Brennan. He closed his bedroom door and called Lorelei. They talked for a bit, and he returned to the living room after 15 minutes.

"Hey, listen," Brennan began. "Problem solved...Lorelei said Clay and his friends can just go to the beach house after the show."

"And will he be coming back here before we go to Florida?" I asked.

"No, he will stay with Lorelei at their house," Brennan began. "Oh, and she did say that when she bought the tickets, Omicron wasn't a thing...and that she was sorry for the trouble."

"Yeah, Omicron wasn't a thing, but COVID has been a thing for almost 21 months now," I fired back. "I mean, I get that she doesn't really care about this pandemic at all since she's had the virus twice now...but I would really like to remain safe when it's within my control to limit my exposure. And yes, we're getting on a plane for the first time in forever next weekend, but we'll be triple-masked, loaded up on our supplement regimen, and generally just as cautious as we have been to date."

Brennan walked past me, muttering, "I did what I could do, and it's fixed now."

"Fine," I acknowledged.

The concert came and went, and Clay went down the shore after the show with his buddies for a night, then back to his mother's primary house, an all-too-close, 20-minute drive from our apartment. But boy, oh boy, did Clay let Brennan have it three days later.

"I am so pissed off at you," the teenager shouted over the phone at Brennan, who decided to take the call from his room with the door closed. I couldn't hear most of the conversation, which went on for more than 20 minutes, but Brennan did call forth his Dad voice for a good part of it. That part I could hear.

"Clay!" Brennan shouted. "I made the right decision based on all the facts I had at the time. Jordyn and I are going to visit Nana and Papa on Christmas Day. Do you really think it would be fair for us to make them sick because you went to a rap concert and came back with COVID? I mean, really, Clay. We, of course, would test before getting on a plane, but there is an incubation period, Son. I made the right decision for everyone. You got to go to a concert you really wanted to see with your buddies. Period."

No mention of my still-healing brain, but whatever. The point was hopefully made and taken. But wait...nope. After a few more minutes, Clay started back up.

"Clay, I am done talking about this with you," Brennan began again. "I did what I thought was best for everyone. It's done. Yes, you will be with your mother for longer over break now, get over it. It was your choice to go to the concert. These are the ramifications for doing so. I will give you your gifts outside for a few minutes on Christmas Eve, and then you can stay with me after we get back."

While Clay was a staunch defender of his mother to anyone outside of his immediate family, the teenager got wise to her several years ago. Brennan had played the mediator for 459 knock-down-drag-out fights between Clay and Lorelei that took place between Clay's junior high years and now. I stood by, shaking my fool head at each one. By age 18, Clay had had enough of his mother's narcissistic ways. Somehow, he managed to survive her beating him with a shoe at age 12, the bribes to kiss her in exchange for money so that she could take a selfie of the kiss for her Facebook page, and giving up his playroom so that she could rent it out to a man for $500/month...even though that man was only there perhaps 3-5 nights each month.

I, too, was divorced, but we had never had children. And we were grownups about everything. I took what was mine, left him what was his, and we settled our debt before I left. And we still wished each other happy birthday via text each year since our divorce. That was the extent of our communication, but at least it was pleasant and kind. I mean, neither of us had cheated, neither of us was abusive, neither of us wished the other ill will. We were just two relatively good people who weren't good together anymore.

So this nonsense that I endured for the last 7.5 years was...well, let's just say I preferred brain surgery. At least I was knocked out for that, and I didn't remember a thing. I wished I could say the same about the crap I put up with. Lorelei never knew which weekends she was supposed to have Clay, nor did she care. She would simply buy tickets to whatever trip, concert, or event she wanted, then she would TELL Brennan that she was going to said event and that Brennan would be responsible for Clay from this day until that day. Conversely, when Brennan and I wanted to take a trip or see a concert, I would check the calendar on my phone (because I figured someone should know when and where Clay would be at all times) to see if it would be Brennan's or Lorelei's weekend with Clay. If it happened to be a weekend where Brennan would have had Clay, I made sure that Brennan asked Lorelei if they could switch weekends before we made our plans or bought tickets for anything. Reciprocity never happened...not once. She simply did not care if it was her designated weekend to have Clay; if she inconvenienced Brennan/me, so be it. If we had to cancel a weekend trip because of her (which happened repeatedly), or if I had to go to my 25th high school reunion by myself after Brennan had already promised me he'd go with me...too damn bad.

It all happened without apology, without remorse, without responsibility taken. However, in fairness, Brennan hardly ever told Lorelei about the canceled plans, the lost money, the arguments between Brennan and me–all because of her lack of common courtesy. But I do not believe it would have mattered. Lorelei cared about one thing in this world—Lorelei. And by God, she was going to get hers. And his. And mine.

Yeah, mine. When Brennan struggled to pay his half the rent, the $1000/month in support, and for fixes to his broken down Land Rover, I had no choice but to help him. I mean, he needed to get to work to have money for at least some of those bills. The kicker—and man, what a kicker—was that while I was laying out money for the mechanic, gas, food, and more...Lorelei thought it would be a great idea to show off how well she was doing "on her own," how she was a self-made, single mom, how with all of her hard work in a pyramid scheme business, so she could afford new Jimmy Choos. She regularly posted pictures on her Facebook page of her new designer shoes and purses, her new Lexuses and Jaguars, and her $1M beach house as dangling carrots in an effort for others to join her team. Lorelei was a pro at taking money from everyone's pocket.

The debate over whether or not Brennan should have allowed Clay to come back to our place eventually died down, and several days later, Brennan and I safely traveled to Florida to see his parents.

We had an OK trip...Florida is not a place I willingly choose to go. When you are a naturally-curly-haired girl, Florida is always a bad hair day. In hindsight, everything was just a bit off during that week. Brennan was fairly distant and cold to me. He was lovely and warm to his parents, but with me, he was markedly different. And his mother was a bit the same. A few of her remarks took me aback, and when I mentioned them to Brennan, he blew it off. It took me 7.5 years to realize it, but Brennan's family—Mom, Dad, Brennan, and Sister—all preferred not to address problems. In good Irish fashion, they simply ignored them. If it meant having an uncomfortable conversation with someone, standing up to someone, or rocking the boat, forget it. They much preferred keeping the peace, even if they knew it wasn't the right thing to do.

I took a daytrip to Sanibel Island by myself. Brennan refused to go, and I didn't want to ask his parents to drive me. So I slipped out while his parents were still in bed and Ubered there and back. It was a delightful day. Brennan and I had one nice night on that trip. On New Year's Eve, we went to a local outdoor pub. His smile seemed genuine for the first time all week.

When Brennan and I returned home, I went back to work full-time on the first Monday of the new year. I had a new lease on life and was full of hope for a better 2022 than my 2021. I mean, it couldn't have been worse than 2021.

7

∿

Chapter 7: The Year of New

January 2022

On January 3, Brennan dropped me off at my office for my first full day of work since mid-September 2021. It felt good to be around my work people again. I never really had a good chance to get to know the new boss of our department, as he only started a few weeks before my seizure. The former CDO who had hired me–seemingly against the wishes of a department of people who were all 15-20 years younger than me—retired in July 2021. But on his way out, he promoted my colleague three levels from specialist to director. She was then my new direct supervisor. I knew before my seizure that this arrangement was headed nowhere fast, but after September 17, I had no options but to endure it, given my medical circumstances.

Day 1 went fine, and I was glad to see some colleagues and friends. Days 2 and 3 were spent working from home, and I was glad to be in a good rhythm again. Feeling productive, if not a little tired, I muscled through each day, working on my tasks and reports.

On Tuesday, my supervisor asked if I could come into the office on Thursday to go over some new roles and responsibilities with our CDO and her. So on Thursday, Brennan dropped me off at the office, and I plowed through some responsibilities until 2 p.m., when I met with my boss and her boss–the relatively new guy.

They had booked the Board Room, even though it was just the three of us. The two of them sat across the gigantic table from me...it was all rather formal. Jacob began the meeting by saying he wanted to thank me for my service...after that, I kinda went into a little trance for a bit, as I knew the rest of what was coming. I just couldn't believe it. This was Day 4 back after medical leave for removal of a brain tumor. Jacob droned on about things like a departmental reorganization, new needs, new positions, and lastly that my position was being eliminated.

Ahhhh, yes, there it was. I was waiting for those words. He continued, "So, we are going to make your last day January 31. Do you have any questions?"

In my head, yes, I had a whole host of questions. But my sister had been in HR her whole career, and I knew enough not to say what I was thinking. Things along the lines of *"After more than 25 years of professional marketing and communications experience, 15 of which have been in the nonprofit world, I'm wondering exactly what it is that you think I can't do for this organization that doesn't even invest in email accounts for all of its employees...that has no budget for marketing...that just can't seem to be great because its purse strings are tied up in wage limitations by the Government?"*

But instead, I said, "No, not just yet. Thank you."

"Alright, I can understand it's a lot to process," Jacob continued. "I just wanted to make sure you knew that this was nothing that you did wrong. You've done a great job here for us, but we simply have different needs now. And this is a difficult decision we had to make, but I will happily write you a letter of recommendation if you ever want one."

"I understand," I replied calmly. "I know these situations are hard for everyone. I do not intend to make it any harder by throwing a tantrum. I'm a professional. I will go quietly."

"Thank you, Jordyn. I do appreciate your maturity in what is a tough spot for all of us," Jacob replied with what appeared to be a genuine sentiment, although I disagreed about the difficulty on their end. It seemed pretty swift and easy to dismiss me after just three full-time days back on the job.

I asked a colleague for a ride home that day, to save Brennan a trip during his work day. When I got to our front door, I took a deep breath in preparation for the conversation ahead. Not having an income was not something either of us was prepared for, but I guess that most people feel that way when it happens to them. And with that, I turned the key, then the knob, and crossed the threshold of an apartment for which I was soon not going to be able to pay my share.

"Hey," I said, as Brennan looked up from his chair. "How was your day?"

"Pretty normal," Brennan began. "Nothing out of the ordinary. How was Day #3? What was the big meeting about today?"

"Well, it wasn't good," I hinted. As his face got a little scrunched up and his head cocked to one side like a curious puppy, I continued. "My position was eliminated today," I said dejectedly, looking at the floor.

"What?!" Brennan asked, disbelievingly. "Seriously?"

"Yes, seriously." I replied. I managed to lift my head to look at his face. "I'm sorry."

"Did they give you a reason?" Brennan asked. "Effective immediately?"

"They said they are reorganizing and that my position is being eliminated," I said. "But no, my last day is January 31."

"OK, what did you say when they told you?" he asked.

"Not much," I replied. "Said I wasn't going to make a fuss about anything, and Jacob thanked me for my maturity. Whatever."

"So you have a month to start looking around, and we can plan for things," Brennan said. "You'll be able to apply for Unemployment, right? That's something. And I can cover the rest of the rent and expenses...you can pay for your car and phone, and whatever is left can go to rent. We'll be fine."

Those words managed to lift the two-ton elephant called 'job loss' off of my chest for the time being. Being granted that grace by Brennan helped a lot in that moment.

With that, Brennan poured both of us a glass of wine, and we assumed our usual positions in the living room for the night. I wasn't sure how much company I would be that night, but Brennan, as usual, was more than happy to fill any dead air with talk of whatever soccer news was happening at the moment or at the very least some tunes from his iPod or my Spotify account.

I might have been able to remain calm at the office, but as everything settled into my bones, I got angry...like, Incredible Hulk angry. And I let it out.

"Who does that Millennial know-it-all bitch think she is?" I started. "I mean, I know she understands the industry, but if I have to change one more &^%#^@$ semicolon to a comma, I might lose my mind. I have tried to explain clauses and sentence structure to her, but it's like I'm speaking Aramaic or something!" I shouted.

"Listen, let's just relax tonight," said Brennan. "If I didn't know better, I'd think you were still taking your Levetiracetam...maybe just take a pause. Everything is going to be fine."

Ugh...the comment about my anti-seizure medicine made me even more upset. From September 18 til mid-December, I had been taking an anti-seizure drug called Levetiracetam. One of the unfortunate side effects for me, as well as those around me, was irritability. The running joke at our place was that the drug should have been named "Levetirace**tantrum**." And I'd be the first to admit it totally made my already limited patience practically non-existent, and I could go from hero to zero in six seconds. And I knew it was a source of contention between us. But I felt a little bit better since weaning off the med, although I don't think Brennan thought my temper had improved that much.

"Hey, you remember that Clay is coming to stay next week, right?" asked Brennan.

"Ummm, yeah, I do now," I responded. "What are the COVID rules next week?"

"What do you mean?" Brennan asked, both of us a bit annoyed now.

"You know what I mean," I retorted. "Will he be running around with all of his college friends and his high school girlfriend each night before he comes back here to sleep?"

"You know he has a very small bubble of friends, and they do not run around and go out to eat like you think," Brennan shot back.

"Yes, of course," I said, the sarcasm dripping from my chin. "They are the exception to their age group for COVID protocol behavior. And his girlfriend goes to high school every day and is exposed to God knows what all day long."

"What do you want me to do, Jordyn? He is at an age where it's important for him to socialize. It's important for the development of his brain."

"Uh-huh...and what about my brain, Brennan?" I fired back. "You know, the one that's still healing from a traumatic injury?"

Brennan ignored the question, walked past me, and closed his bedroom door after entering. I pulled out my phone and pulled up the AirBnB app. I just remembered that I promised my good friend, Lee, that I would come stay with her next Friday after her surgery. She had been a huge support throughout my ordeal—from providing hospital guidance to giving me rides to and from outpatient therapy sessions to a few follow-up doctor visits—Lee was a rockstar friend. And now it was my turn to repay her kindnesses by staying with her for a night after her surgery.

When Brennan reemerged from his room, I took the opportunity to run my proposal for next week past him.

"Hey, I found an AirBnB for next week for me to stay in," I said. He looked confused. "You remember that Lee is getting her surgery next week, right? And that I am staying with her on Friday night?" I asked.

"Oh, yeah, right," he confirmed. "So what's the deal with the AirBnB?"

"Well, if Clay is going to be here and seeing his friends each night, I cannot risk exposing Lee to COVID when she has just had surgery," I explained. "So I will stay in an AirBnB next week to make sure that both she and I are as safe as possible."

"Ok, that makes sense," Brennan agreed.

"Yeah, I thought so," I said. "And if you are agreeable, I'd like for you to pay for it. I have paid for half of Clay's food for 7.5 years, half of the utilities he used every other weekend and two nights per week, and you never contributed any extra towards the rent, despite having the master bedroom with ensuite bath so that Clay could have privacy and not have to walk five steps across a hall to use the other bathroom."

Brennan thought for five seconds, then agreed to my terms. "Sure, that's fine. How much is it? Just pay out of the joint account, and I'll move money into it to cover the cost."

"It's $500 for the entire week," I told him.

"Done," said Brennan as he pulled out his phone and moved the money into our joint account. Since changing jobs three years prior into the Pharma space, he no longer had a cash flow issue. And now that he just switched companies, he was making even more.

Monday morning I packed up my bag and work laptop for the week and made the 25-minute trek to old stomping grounds in an effort to remain safe during the week for my friend to whom I owed a huge debt of gratitude. The spot was in a cool, old building with several apartments in it, and mine was on the second floor. It was cute, not a lot of frills, but I did not need frills, I only needed some space to be safe. Oddly, there were two window air-conditioning units in two of the windows, one in the dining room and one in my bedroom. And unfortunately, they did not have a tight fit or seal, which proved problematic and really, really cold in early January. I slept with extra layers of clothes on for the first two nights, but come Tuesday, I needed to be warmer. Then I remembered I had a space heater at home in my room that doubled as a fan. I never needed the heater at home, but I certainly needed it in that AirBnB.

The whole situation of my feeling like I needed to leave because of Brennan's lack of control and Clay's lack of empathy started to really irritate me. In my mind, the two of them should have been the ones to leave the apartment...not me. I was still abiding by our rules. They were not. As I stewed in my own bile a bit, I decided to do something bold, different, and perhaps out of character.

It had been a while since Brennan and Lorelei had had a big blowout, even though she and Clay had them on an every-few-days schedule. The reason Clay wanted to be at our place was because he and his mother fought about the silliest, dumbest, and most inane things. In the grand scheme of things, these were big, fat, nothing donuts. Like the fact that Clay did not take the dogs out for the 14th time that day, or that he did not respond to her calling his name because he had his headphones on in his room while she was in the basement, or that he hadn't cleaned up his room when she had asked him to.

So, I did this thing. I called Lorelei. I mean, it wasn't like I had never spoken to her before. Over the years, there were several short conversations on the sidelines of a soccer pitch about things like whether Clay left his cleats at her place or ours, along with text conversations about her need to read the text messages that I sent to Clay (when she would take his phone as punishment for his smart mouth) about peanut butter and jelly sandwiches for an upcoming beach trip. And according to Brennan, She had been asking how I was doing while I stared down death a few months ago. I actually texted her first to see if she could talk. She was on a business call just then, but she said she'd call me when she was finished.

"Hello, this is Jordyn," I said when she called 20 minutes later.

"Hi, Jordyn," she said excitedly.

"Hi, Lorelei, thanks for calling."

"Sure thing. I know you have something you want to talk about, but first, tell me...how are you doing?" Lorelei sounded sincere and genuine, to my surprise.

"I am doing well, thanks."

"Brennan was keeping me up to date on your surgeries and all," she replied. "Are you feeling good now?"

We exchanged pleasantries for quite some time, then when an appropriate amount of them had gone back and forth, I started with the purpose of my call.

"Lorelei, I'm actually in an AirBnB this week because Clay is staying with us, but because I do not know where he goes at night or who he sees or if he is being cautious, I am here in a freezing cold apartment, as I have promised to stay with a friend who is having surgery later this week. And I just cannot in good conscience go and unwittingly expose her to COVID if Clay were to bring it back to our place. My friend was a superstar during my ordeal, and I owe her this."

"Of course, I completely understand," she said. "What do you need from me?"

"Well, if there is any way at all that you and Clay could get along a bit better, I would not be in this situation," I cautiously posited. "He wanted to stay with us because the two of you fight often, according to Clay."

"Oh, Jordyn, I am sorry you are in this spot, and that you are the one to be in that AirBnB," Lorelei sympathized. "I, too, wish he and I could get along better."

And for the next 1.5 hours, the ex-wife of my partner of almost eight years and I spoke calmly, rationally, honestly about Clay, Brennan, her relationship with Clay, and what we might be able to do to make their situation better. One of the two highlights from that conversation included finding out that Brennan had never once, in 7.5 years, told Lorelei that he and I were in a committed relationship until I was lying in a hospital bed and might never use the left side of my body again. When she asked Brennan about me after my October surgeries, he told her that he might have to figure out how to care for me if I never moved my left side again. Lorelei asked why that responsibility would fall on him if we were just roommates...why wouldn't my family be responsible.

Brennan's response apparently was "Well, I care about her a lot. We're in a relationship."

The next major topic of discussion was a possible solution to the Clay-Lorelei butting of heads. I suggested that the four adults in Clay's life–Brennan, Lorelei, James, and me all sit down and talk about ways to make this better for everyone. Lorelei was totally on board, and she was confident that James would be, too. In fact, he was sitting in the next room while we talked, so she just asked him right then and there. Sure enough, James had no issue with trying to have a happier home life with his newly minted family of just over a year. He also had two children from a wife who had passed away not long before he married Lorelei.

So the only one left to convince was Brennan. I crossed my fingers and called him.

"You did WHAT?" Brennan screamed through the phone. "How dare you call my ex-wife? And why would you think that SHE would be able to do anything about this? You are talking to the wrong person, Jordyn."

"Well, Brennan, I've tried talking to you, asking you to try to fix things between Clay and me for four years now, and you've done nothing. So I figured I would go to the source of the issue."

"You have betrayed me," he snarled at me. "And I will never sit down and talk about my son with the three of you. This does not involve you."

"The hell it doesn't," I came back at him. "I live in that place, too. I pay half the rent, half the food, half the utilities—all things that Clay partakes in, yet never acknowledges. And he certainly does not respect me when he does speak."

"I just don't understand why you thought calling her would help," he said.

"I was trying to save our relationship, Brennan," I finally said. "We're slipping away from each other, and I did the only thing I could think to do."

"Well, you thought wrong," he snapped. "Instead of saving us, you killed us." And with that he hung up.

Oh, shit. I never saw that coming. It was almost noon, and I had a 12:45 chiropractor appointment about two miles from our apartment. After my adjustment, I decided to stop by the apartment to pick up the space heater. When I got to the door, I fumbled for my key, and just before I put it in the knob, I heard Brennan and Clay speaking inside the entryway. I stopped to listen.

"Listen, Dude," Brennan said to his son. "Sometimes when you call, Jordyn knows we're talking about important stuff, and she asks what is going on."

"Well, can't you lie?" Clay suggested.

"I can't always deflect with her," Brennan started. "Sometimes I just have to tell her what's going on because she knows that something is up."

I shook my head to myself in the hallway. *Did I really just hear my partner tell his 18-year-old son that it is OK to lie to one's significant other? Is that really what just happened? This from the man who had sworn he had never lied to me the way he did to his ex-wife?*

"Oh, and you should know," Brennan started up again. "Jordyn called your mother today to talk."

"Well, I don't like that one bit!" Clay shot back.

And with that, I could take no more, and I put the key in the hole, turned the knob and blew into the apartment like a gale force wind.

"Well," I said, staring directly at Clay, "there are a lot of things that I don't like." Then I blew past them to my room, grabbed my space heater, and beelined back to the front door, shooting a sinister glare at Brennan as I slammed the door behind me as hard as I possibly could. I think people on the four floors below us felt the impact.

After I got back to my AirBnB, I texted Brennan, and we went back and forth for a few minutes. At the end of the thread, he texted.

Brennan: I think when you get a new job,
we should live apart. This is not working.

I could not believe what I just read.

Me: Did you just break up with me?
Are we done?

Brennan: Call it what you want,
but yes, we are done.

Me: You know what, Brennan? I just realized it would have been easier for you if I had just died on the operating table.

Brennan: F@%* YOU for saying
that! That would not have been
better.

Me: I didn't say better, I said easier. That way, you would not have had to come up with some lie to tell your family about why we are not together anymore.

I decided to try to be an adult, so I called him. But he did not answer. I called again...same non-answer. He eventually texted that he did not want to speak to me for a few days.

In the next two days, I had researched, visited, and secured an apartment in Lancaster County, where Brennan and I had put in two bids on houses in September before my seizure, but we were outbid by tens of thousands of dollars. I had lived in Lancaster for five years in the early 2000s, and it had always felt like home. And right then, I wanted...no, I **needed** to go home. Because my home, my sanctuary, my safe place had just been taken from me. I was no longer wanted in the home Brennan and I created together. And I certainly couldn't stay in a place where I wasn't speaking to or enjoying the person I was living with. That was no home at all.

8

Ɔ∾

Chapter 8: When Drowning, Look for Love Preservers

On my first trip to Lancaster, I found my new apartment in front of a gorgeous pond—which in turn, sat in front of a farm with a big black horse, several may-awing peacocks, a herd of goats, some wild turkeys, and one "Randy the Rooster." My friend from a lifetime ago offered to have me stay with her and her family in Lancaster that night.

"Jordyn, you've been through a lot," Cathy said. "Please, come and stay here tonight. Jason is away on business, and the girls would love to have someone new to talk to."

Since I wasn't exactly relishing the thought of another shivering night in the drafty AirBnB, I said 'yes.'

It only took one night for me to fall very much in love with Cathy's youngest daughter, the adorably bespectacled Emma. At just seven years young, this little intuitive feeler found a kindred spirit in me. That night, when Cathy put her to bed, as Emma snuggled into her blankets, she said to her mother, "Mom, I really like Jordyn."

"You do?" asked Cathy.

"Yes," affirmed the sweet girl. "Could you go downstairs and ask her if she likes your kids?"

Oh. My. Goodness. I almost cried on the spot when Cathy came back downstairs to tell me what Emma had said. She also apparently asked if I could stay with them a little while longer. And just like that, I had a place of warmth and refuge for the next month until my apartment was ready. I would not have to tiptoe around awkwardness, aka Brennan, nor live in a space where I knew I was not really welcome.

Graciously, thankfully, and willingly I found sanctuary, a safe space, a temporary home to feel a part of for the next 30 days. I did my very best to be a good guest—helping to buy groceries, to wash and fold the laundry, to do dishes, to pick up takeout, to watch the girls on Valentine's weekend, to keep my space and bathroom (which the girls gave up for me) clean.

One Saturday morning during my stay, Jason knocked on my door, asked if I was decent, and then delivered my first-ever breakfast in bed! Homemade pancakes, orange juice, water, and a little jug of maple syrup. Which, when I posted the picture to Facebook, was noticed by my long-lost college friend, Nate. And he remarked that his cousin made that syrup. I mentioned it to Cathy the next day, and she shook her head in slight disbelief and said, "My cousin made that syrup!" My two friends were cousins!

And I began another reconnection to "home." Lebanon Valley College always felt like home, even when I was homesick my freshman year, even after I had returned for alumnae volleyball matches, and especially on the night I was invited to sit across a special table from my college head coach and his wife, my assistant coach, for his Hall of Fame induction. Sometimes home is a place, but I was quickly confirming that more often than not, home is people. No matter how much time had passed between actual conversations, Wayne and Diana were some of my favorite people.

While I stayed at Cathy's house, Wayne and I embarked on a special mission that played into his retired hands...to make a resin river table for my new dining room. We drove to State College, hand-picked a slab of wood, and for the next three months, Wayne worked on perfecting a stunningly beautiful heirloom-quality table for my new home...so that I could gather friends and family around a table to enjoy good food, make good memories, and be grateful for every good moment in a life that was still good, despite some recent bad events.

And then, in the very, very early morning of my 49th birthday, just days before Cathy & family's Disney vacation and my move into my own space, I walked downstairs to prepare a cup of tea, and I stopped dead in my tracks as I saw the dining room had been prepared for a party...my party. There were pastel streamers and balloons all around, a happy birthday sign had been strung over the fireplace mantle, and the table was set for the dinner we had spoken about from my favorite Mexican place in Lancaster. My mouth went agape, my hand covered my mouth, and tears rolled down. No one had thrown me a birthday party since I turned 30, and I love a good birthday party, no matter whose it is. Especially when there are surprises. And this part was definitely a surprise.

In another surprise, Cathy and Jason, who were both HR professionals for most of their careers, encouraged me to file suit regarding my job loss. They both spoke with exaggerated enthusiasm, arms flailing about and loud voices, "Jordyn, this case is a slam dunk! There's your age, your medical condition, and the fact that you just came back from FMLA, not to mention the emails from your boss about your 'mental state.' Seriously, Jordyn, look into talking to an employment lawyer," both of them said pretty much the exact same thing.

And with their extreme votes of confidence behind me, I did just that. I lost my partner of eight years, my home of eight years, and a job...all within the course of one week. And I almost lost my life twice, three months prior. What else did I possibly have to lose?

After two calls, I found a crackpot lawyer who worked some employment law magic, and I received four months of pay, plus four months of paid healthcare. That gave me a bit of breathing room, a bit of space to find a job, and a bit of time to maybe create some income for myself.

By March 2022, I had launched a little website, Facebook page, and charcuterie board business. The foodie rage that had swept the country was something that I had loved to do for Brennan and me. I would create boards of meats, cheeses, nuts, spreads, chocolates, crackers, and more for our dinners from time to time, and he loved them. So I figured, why not?

And I began creating little spreads for people to enjoy, as hospitality was a gift that came naturally to me. From a giant Easter Egg bowl for my dear friend's three boys to a pizza board for the lovely handlers who helped my college coaches carry my gorgeous finished table up into my apartment, I had a blast trying to drum up business in my new-again home county by posting pictures and stories about the food gifts I presented to my friends.

One of my few sales came from one of my oldest and dearest friends from high school. She still lived in our hometown, one county west, and she had just moved in with her boyfriend who had an upcoming birthday. So she asked me to do charcuterie for the party, which I happily obliged. Mis and I were both hustling to make ends meet, and she wanted to support one of my side gigs while taking some work off her own plate for the party. Doing a party for friends took just a little bit of the pressure off, which was really nice! I also went the extra mile for them as well, providing more food than I was paid to.

I enjoyed being much closer to my longtime friend. It made getting together for a meal, drinks, or a party so much easier. And last-minute plans were totally an option now. It was funny to me how being in closer physical proximity meant we spoke more on the phone as well, especially in and at an age where virtually everyone was far too busy with their own stuff to find much time to hang out with friends. Most people had children, grandchildren, a significant other, and/or parents with failing health to deal with on top of a household, job, and bills. All I had at that moment was bills, and plenty of them. But Mis and I worked at getting together, paying attention to important dates on each other's calendars, and checking in on tough days. We both had plenty of tough-day burdens whose loads we could share, and somehow, the burdens were much more bearable that way...even though they weren't gone.

There was something super comforting about a worn-in love preserver...one who knew all your darkest deeds and still loved you in spite of them. That was a love preserver to be cherished, cared for, and kept close.

In early June, fueled by a burning desire to reconnect, reconnect, reconnect with more friends from what felt like a lifetime ago, I held a reunion for the friends I had made at what I still called my "home church," even though I had not attended for many years. After the pastor, whom I loved so dearly, had passed away from a heart ailment during the pandemic, I "attended" his online service at Zion UMC, to mourn his death with family and friends, and to be reminded that "the best was yet to be."

Our "small group" of 20-ish friends piled into my apartment with the intent of going outside to gather around the pond and sing tunes from our old blue song books, cook on the grills provided by my apartment complex, and generally just enjoy the serenity in which I landed. However, we never made it outside. Everyone just congregated around my amazing table, snacked on charcuterie bounty, laughed at photos circa 1998-2000, and relived old memories. Friends brought side dishes to share, I poured glasses of bubbly for a toast to "old friends who had been away too long" from one another's company, and we all took pictures for the next reunion. And we laughed. We hugged. We looked at one another like long-lost brothers and sisters...who had some gray hairs, some extra pounds, some wrinkles, and some scars. We all knew that we didn't get to be this age without some battle wounds. But we were amongst friends, and none of that mattered on that day. We were there, we were not treading water on this day, we were simply floating in and on love. We were love preservers, on a summer day in June 2022.

It was indeed good to be home.

About two weeks later, the wife of one of my love preservers, contacted me about doing a charcuterie spread for a party they were having for the members of their gym. Jeremiah had a ginormous heart for his tribe—for those who struggled with anything, for those who were authentically, unapologetically themselves, for those who tried on the daily to be a better version of themselves than they were the day before. And he had always felt like "home" to me. Maybe because we wrestled with the same struggles from time to time, but definitely because we loved an authentic person with the cheese falling off his crackers who was also a beautiful writer named Brennan Manning (not to be confused with my ex-partner, Brennan).

So when Kim, Jeremiah's wife, called to ask me to do a big spread for a Summer Solstice party for the members of the gym that they owned, I was thrilled. Jeremiah texted me the day of the party, inviting me to stay and enjoy the party after I had set everything up. I wasn't really sure about that, but when I got to the member's house where the party was being held, I decided I could stay for a few minutes. The charcuterie boards were a hit, and there was a pool, cornhole, and lots of fun conversations happening. As a former athlete with a modicum of ability left in her, I took up the cornhole challenge a few times–once with Jeremiah, who apparently should play professionally, if there is such a thing, and plenty of times against him. Typically known for being a good loser and good sport, I might have pushed him in the pool after his third win against me. However, I told him I was prepared for retaliation, just as soon as I removed the phone from my pocket. He never reciprocated, but he did continue to win. And the competitor in me rallied his gym employees and members to put an end to his reign of dominance. It never happened. Jeremiah remained undefeated all night.

When it looked like the party was dying down, I started to round up my empty-ish boards and put leftovers in containers for Kim to take home with her. One of their gym members was in the kitchen with me as I was tidying and packing up. I introduced myself, and Ryan and I began chatting about his background, his love of...er...obsession with running, and his church. He told me that I should come visit sometime. So I asked for details and said that I might come the next morning.

Thirteen hours later, I showered, dressed, and made my way to the southeast quadrant of Lancaster city, to a little area known as Church-towne, because well, there were quite a few churches within a baseball's throw from one another. This church happened to meet in a community center, and when I walked in, it looked just like a community center does almost anywhere...cinder block walls, kitchen off to one side, and a gym in the back. I looked around and spied Ryan. He greeted me, said he was glad I came, and sat down with me on folding chairs at a folding table with a plastic tablecloth over top of it. This was known as Brunch Church...every week they served a free pancake breakfast while church happened. I loved the concept. Jesus was all about sharing food with friends and people who would become his friends. Right on...let's see what you got, Brunch Church.

The pastor introduced herself shortly after 10 a.m., as people were still coming in and getting some pancakes and coffee. Little kids walked around with pancakes spilling out the sides of their tiny hands. All the while sticky, little smiles lit up their faces. Soon a small worship team walked to the front of the room, words to a song appeared on the screen behind them, and we began to sing songs that were new to me. I had been away from church and church tunes for a long time. But the most interesting part of that worship time was that some of the songs we sang were in languages other than English–intentionally. One was in Spanish, one was in Swahili, and several in English. There weren't many people of color there that morning, but it was the hope of this church to eventually look like the community in which it was planted.

I was dumbfounded...a church that walks the talk? Could it be? In a poor, little neighborhood south of Lancaster City square. Yes, what could be more perfect? I was about to find out.

The pastor began to give her message, which was based in Jeremiah, specifically Jeremiah 29. I chuckled to myself, as I had recently ordered a canvas print that I had designed with one of my sunrise photos from Florida. Laid overtop of the picture were the words from Jeremiah 29:11-13. Yes, it is one of the masses' most beloved verses, and one of mine as well. And here I was for the first time in years, in a church, where the sermon being preached was from my favorite Bible verse.

"Ummmm, OK, God," I thought silently. "You have my attention...again. I'm listening."

I met with the pastor that week, shared the crazy story of the past year with her, and she prayed with me. I also left some materials for her from when I owned my own marketing business. I had worked with several churches to help with campaigns, logo designs, brochures, and branding. I had also worked with a pastor she knew to create an Advent devotional. In the event she liked any of the material, I wanted to offer it as a jumping off point for anything there at Brunch Church.

I continued to visit the church, and Ryan and I became fast friends, despite our almost 20-year age gap. On the day after his 30th birthday, we continued the celebration by crossing off a bucket-list item for Ryan...going axe-throwing. I had created another charcuterie board spread for him and his friends, complete with a birthday cake that met his allergy restrictions. We had a blast, and since I did some free marketing for the axe-throwing meadery where we had his party, they gave us some extra-special attention, including a gigantic axe with which Ryan cut his cake and pretended to lick the blade. It was a shindig fit for a king...or at least a Viking...a 30-year-old, long-distance-running Viking.

When Ryan learned I was a lover of words, a writer, and a grammar freak, he shared his mother's blog about encouragement for living, called Little Life Words. So I signed up to receive her weekly posts, all of which seemed to be written just for me. I donated a few bucks here and there to her worthy work, and I would send a reply each Monday after reading her powerful words and listening to the song she would share. I'd send a note of thanks, sometimes how the message touched me that week, and I'd send a song back to her around the same theme. We did this for a few weeks, and then I learned that she was a spiritual director. I emailed Jenny to ask if she would be willing to work with me, as I certainly needed some guidance from a well-intentioned person. Jenny let me know that her roster was full up, but that we could share a cup of tea sometime.

One year to the day after the fateful day in my kitchen that changed my life forever, I met with Jenny. The lovely, kind, gentle fellow writer listened with an empathetic ear as I poured out the contents of my heart at a picnic table outside a local coffee shop. Within a few minutes of chatting, I could see that Ryan got his sweet disposition honestly.

Jenny continued to post to her blog, and I continued to read. About four weeks after our tea date, I opened Jenny's blog on a Monday morning to a shock. There in print for the world to read was my name, next to the words, "my new friend." Then she went on to talk about the compassion for others that she saw in me. I was in tears before I finished that paragraph. Someone who had met me in person just once, honestly and truly saw me. She got me, she understood my heart, my desires, my hurts. And she honored them like we had been friends for our entire lives.

How did I manage to find two love preservers in one family? Two friends for a lifetime at a time when I needed them desperately. Two friends who were biological family to one another...two friends who became the family that I was privileged to choose. One friend, now a brother; one friend, now a sister.

9

Chapter 9: God Spelled Backwards

About one month after taking up my new residence, I saw an adorable miniature Shetland sheepdog, known as a mini Sheltie, in my neighborhood. She was so sweet, and the owners let me play with her for a bit. I asked if there were other pups in the litter and if I could have the breeder's name and contact info.

"Yes" and "yes" were the answers. I knew I wasn't ready to have a puppy yet, but it was lonelier than I anticipated being on my own after having a husband and/or partner around for the better part of two decades. Perhaps I could just call the breeder to see if I could get a pup from the next litter.

So I called Katelyn, who lived in Ohio, to get some information. Unfortunately, the mother was her pet, and she had already had three litters. Katelyn was not in the business of running a puppy mill, so she would not be breeding her again anytime soon, if at all. Also, there was only one puppy left out of the litter.

<<Sigh.>>

If I wanted a mini Sheltie that looked like Rey, my neighbor's puppy, I would have to act fast.

Three days later, I was on my way to Pittsburgh to pick up Finnegan. Katelyn and her sister agreed to meet me on the western edge of Pittsburgh to save me four hours of a roundtrip to bring him home. He was just too adorable, tiny, and sweet. He was on a short leash and would wander shyly between Katelyn's legs.

Eventually, it was time to make the four-hour trip home. I put Finnegan in the hard-case carrier for safety as I was traveling by myself. He did pretty well, despite not being a fan of the carrier.

I had decided before I went to get Finn that I would not allow him to sleep in my bed with me. He would sleep in the carrier. When we reached my apartment and rounded the corner, I saw that his sister, Rey, was outside with her humans. So I parked, got Finnegan out and on leash, and we walked down the sidewalk towards Rey. I was super anxious to see if the puppies would recognize one another. When Finn saw Rey, he tugged at his leash to get closer to her. And after a few sniffs from both of them, they both began playfully romping and barking. It was just what I had hoped for! Finn would be able to play with his sister regularly! What could be better?

We eventually pulled the brother and sister apart, and Finn and I went inside for his first night in his new home. I got everything situated, filled a water bowl and food bowl. I had bought a few toys for him ahead of time, and I had a soft, plush blanket for him.

I put his little bed mat back into his crate around 9 p.m., and I tried to put Finn in the crate again. But he was having no part of that. He refused, wriggled, and whimpered. The dramatics worked. He had already wormed his way onto my bed on Night 1. Katelyn had told me that Finn slept with her and that he liked to snuggle.

So, in the bed he went with me. No whimpering, no pushback, no issues. Just a little circle to find just the right spot, a few inches away from me. He slept well until about 5 a.m. when he wanted to go potty.

And so it began, I was officially a dog mom, and I loved it...and him, despite his constant barking at/herding of me, neighbors, neighbor dogs, and generally any human within eyesight. But I couldn't be too mad at him, as he was simply doing what he was bred to do—keep every living thing in line.

Finnegan was an instant hit in the neighborhood, what with his adorable little face and big brown eyes. My new neighbor-friends, Marjorie and Sylvia, became Finnegan's first aunties. Marjorie was a dog whisperer and took every opportunity to help me try to train Finn, and Sylvia was dubbed "the Hot Dog Lady," as she always carried a baggie of baked hot dogs with her at all times...for all the dogs in the development. Every puppy knew Auntie Sylvia, and Finnegan was no exception.

Three weeks after Finnegan got his forever home, the residents of my apartment complex received a notice from the property management company about a lawn application that would be spread over every bit of grass as far as the eye could see. Essentially, they were paying the lawn care company to spread weed killer on the grass in front of my apartment, in front of and around the pond a few steps from my front door, and on every bit of grass within two stones' throws of my place in two days. Also in the email, was this note:

"Please keep your pets off the grass from 10:30 a.m. - 4:30 p.m. until the grass dries."

My reaction to those words were visceral and immediate.

Although I was not an environmental scientist, I knew several of them...I had worked with several of them...I was married to one. And I knew enough to question what chemicals were being spread across every inch of green in my neighborhood. There was no way I was going to let anyone harm my Finny, whether that be intentional or not.

As soon as the property management company office opened that day, I called and asked to speak with the maintenance manager.

"Hello, this is Jordyn Osborne in Apt B," I began calmly. "I'd like to know the name of the people who will be spreading chemicals over the grass later today."

"It's the same company who does our regular weekly lawn care on Mondays," Stephanie began. "Natural Wonder Landscaping and Lawn Care."

"OK," I replied. "Do you have their phone number? I'd like to speak with them."

"What do you need, Jordyn?" Stephanie retorted.

"I need to find out exactly what is in the poison that will be spread all over the grass," I fired back, not nearly as calmly. "My puppy is just three months old, and I find it ridiculous that you think people's pets should be able to not go to the bathroom for seven hours. And beyond that, I sincerely doubt that it will be safe for my puppy to be on the grass at 4:30 p.m."

"Jordyn, I'm sorry you seem so unhappy here," said Stephanie, seemingly ignoring my question. "If you like, I can see about letting you out of your lease, so that you could look for a place where you'd enjoy living."

Incredulous about what I had just heard, I took a moment, shook it off, and said, "May I have Normal Wonder's phone number, please?"

"I don't have it at my fingertips, Jordyn," Stephanie replied.

"Never mind. I will look it up," I managed to sigh out. And then I hung up.

When I rang Natural Wonder's number, I spoke with one of the owners, an Amishman named Amos. "Hi, Amos, my name is Jordyn Osborne, and I live in the apartment complex where you are scheduled to spread weed killer today," I began politely. "I was wondering if you could tell me what the ingredients in the weed killer are? I have a brand new puppy, Amos, and I am very concerned about what he might be licking off his paws later today."

"Oh, yes, I understand, Jordyn," Amos kindly replied. "I don't blame you. If I had a puppy, I wouldn't want him on the grass after weed killer was spread, either. And you should know, we will be spreading this weed killer six more times this year."

Incredulous once again, I shook my head, wondering to myself what kind of Amishman, or person of any faith at all, could knowingly disseminate potentially harmful chemicals on grass for people to drag into their homes, for pets to get all over their paws and potentially lick. I could feel my blood pressure begin to tick upward.

"I don't have the list at my fingertips, but I can look it up and call you back," Amos said. "Would that be alright?"

"Yes, thank you, Amos," I agreed.

When I received the list of chemicals a few hours later, I began doing my due diligence that afternoon. I looked up every single ingredient, determining my initial assessment was right. The chemicals were not safe for man nor beast, and certainly not for my puppy.

Then I picked up the phone and called the property management company back, this time I asked to speak with Keith, one of the owners. When I had to give my name, I knew I was not going to be put through, so I left a message. A few hours later, I did receive a call back from Keith.

"Hello," I said. "This is Jordyn."

"Hi, Jordyn. This is Keith," the voice on the other end of the line said.

"Thank you for returning my call," I started. "I was hoping I could speak with you for a few moments about the chemicals that Natural Wonder plans to spread all over our grass for six more times this year. You see, Keith, I have a small puppy...one I just paid a lot of money for. And there are lots of other dogs in this neighborhood, as I'm sure you know. We all pay a nice fee each month to your company for the privilege of having a dog. As such, I'd like to make sure I continue to have my dog. And so I would like to propose an alternative idea to you."

"Ok, Jordyn," he said. "I'm listening."

"Well, Keith," I continued. "When I called and spoke to Stephanie about my dissatisfaction with all the chemicals applied to our grass and the ill-effects that they could have on our pets, her solution was to get rid of me...to let me out of my lease. I guess she just didn't want to hear my legitimate concern and figured it would be easier on her to just have me gone."

"I'm sure she didn't mean—" started Keith. However, I wasn't having any of it.

"But I have another solution, Keith. It's quite simple, really. Just rope off a small plot of ground where the chemicals will not be spread until the following week, that way our pups can safely do their business without our fear of their being poisoned. Natural Wonder can bring a hand spreader back for that tiny plot next week...no need for the big machines."

Keith took a moment, then said, "Well, that sounds like a completely reasonable and doable request, Jordyn."

"Yes, I thought so, too, Keith," I agreed. "And it only took me 15 minutes to come up with it. Stephanie could have done the same thing if she had thought about it for a moment...instead of immediately going to guns, telling me I was welcome to live elsewhere, so she wouldn't have to hear my mouth."

"I don't think that's what she meant or intended, Jordyn," assured Keith. "I know what she was trying..."

I cut him off again, "Yes, I know what she was trying to do, too, Keith...and this is a teachable moment from my vantage point."

Keith did not acknowledge that point, but instead wrapped up with, "Thank you for your idea, Jordyn. I will get back to you within a few weeks, after I speak with Amos."

"I have a feeling he will be on board, Keith," I said. "When I mentioned the toxicity of the chemicals to Amos, he instantly agreed with me, saying he would not allow his own puppy on the grass even a day or two after the chemicals went down." And with that, we said our goodbyes.

So, for three full days, I did not let Finnegan on the grass. We tried once at 5 a.m. the next morning to let him pee in the neighbor's yard across the street. The neighbor owned his own home, but he had a big German Shepherd who was just a puppy herself, but she was intimidating to say the least. He left her off leash because there was an electric fence. However, the moment Finnegan stepped onto the first blade of grass, that Shepherd came barrelling out of nowhere, headed straight for Finn and me in the dark before dawn.

I screamed my head off and promptly began to cry, as I yanked Finn back and ran across the street to my development.

The owner of the house and yard came out, and when I told him what we were trying to do, he said it was fine to let Finn pee on the yard. He also said that his pup was just a year old, and that she meant no harm.

I thanked him, but politely declined the offer, as both Finn and I were quite scared.

So for the next two days, we walked some distances for him to do his business. Down over the hill was a path that led through some small woods. We trekked down there multiple times each day. On the third day, I was on the path, talking with another neighbor—who had a cute puppy as well—about my disgust at the weed killer situation. When without warning, a large Boxer came charging around the bend, off leash and headed straight for Finn!

I screamed for the second time in two days about a large, aggressive dog coming after my teeny, tiny Finnegan, who weighed in at a whopping eight pounds, and I instinctively lifted Finn up by his leash so that the Boxer could not get to him. I grabbed Finnegan in my arms, and began running back up the hill towards my apartment. When I rounded the corner of the path, I ran into the owner of the Boxer.

"Oh, my!" she began. "I'm so sorry, he got off leash!"

In my sheer exasperation, I retorted, "I've had ENOUGH! Enough!" And I kept running. In retrospect, it most likely was an accident that her dog got off leash, but I had no time to do anything but react and keep running. Right foot in front of left foot, left foot in front of right foot, repeat, repeat, repeat. And dear Lord, I was so out of shape. I huffed and I puffed, and I conquered the small hill, and finally put Finnegan down on the macadam parking lot.

Finally, we were safe. Safe from other dogs, safe from chemical-laden grass...safe. We went inside the apartment, and we both laid down for a bit.

When the next weed killer application rolled around, and every application thereafter, there was a yellow "caution"-taped-off section of grass that was designated as "safe" for all pups to do their business. Every time I took Finn over there for the next two applications, at least one other dog owner mentioned how nice this was...that our dogs have a place to go without being in chemicals. I would smile and agree. Sometimes I would tell them that I made that happen, and that we could likely get a permanently-fenced off area as a designated dog park if more owners would simply call and ask for one. We all agreed we paid a stupid amount of rent to live there, and that the $50/month per pet could more than cover a chain-link fence with less than one month's rent from 50+ dog-owning tenants.

But people tend not to make waves, even if it is in their best interest, or the best interest of their best friend. They simply take it on the chin, grin, and bear it. That has never been my nature...and oh my, I do love nature. My nature said "stand up for what is right...always. Fight for justice, and do it with all you have." So even if I did it alone, I spoke my truth to power.

#####

Unfortunately, Finnegan didn't get to interact with his sister all that much or for very long. Having one of his siblings close by played such a factor in my getting him at a time when I wasn't financially or physically ready for a puppy, but I did it because I knew he would be close to part of his dog family.

Early on, Rey's humans had smacked her whenever she'd bark so that she no longer did...except when Finn was around, because he'd get all excited to play with his sister, and they'd both bark. Since barking was forbidden for Rey, Finnegan paid the price by not getting to be around his sister. Whenever Finnegan and I would round the corner to Rey's home and she would happen to be outside, her human mother would yank her back inside to avoid letting Rey play with Finn. Dogs really were better than humans most of the time.

Finnegan was my very first dog. And I had always heard about the unconditional love of a dog for his human, and I had watched as my sister got a dog, then another, and another. But I had never experienced it first-hand...until Finn. His little face and big brown eyes lured me in...I would forever be a sucker for my pupper. And I was totally OK with that.

The first time that Finnegan escaped the house was one of the worst feelings of my life. It was a super windy and cold day in October. And when I brought him back in from a potty break, I forgot to turn the deadbolt.

Then I sat down to finish watching a movie. Before I knew it, I was engrossed and had not heard from Finnegan for a while.

"Finn? Finny? Finnegan!!! Where are you???" I shouted.

No response.

So I got up and walked around my tiny place, and finally, I went to the stairs to find an open door at the bottom! WHAT?!?!?!

With no shoes, no bra, no jacket and no phone, I ran up and down the parking lot screaming for Finnegan at the top of my lungs. "Finnegan!!! Finn!!! Finny...COME! Finnegan, where are you?"

A neighbor had just walked through the portico passthrough from the other side of my building. When she saw and heard my distress, she said, "Hi...I believe your puppy is at your neighbor's house around the backside."

"What? Can you show me?" I begged her.

"Sure, come with me," she replied.

As we briskly walked towards the one end of the building, I knew instantly where she was taking me—Auntie Sylvia's house, of course! I didn't even have to knock, Sylvia was opening the door as I approached.

"I was wondering where you were!" she exclaimed. "Finn was out here on my chair, barking...but you were nowhere to be found."

"Yes, he got out when a gale-force wind blew open my door!" I shrieked as I picked up my boy and squeezed him tight. "Don't you ever do that again...never run away again, Finny! You scared Mommy to death!"

Finnegan didn't know he had done anything wrong...all he knew was there was an opening, and he took it. And when he got it, he went straight to Auntie Sylvia's for hot dogs.

This scenario happened again a few months later, when my dad came to visit. When Finnegan saw that I wasn't alone at the door, he bolted outside, and again, went straight for the Hot Dog Lady. At least this time, I knew right away where to look for him. Not nearly as much terror this time, but I still was a bit freaked out. Thank God for Auntie Sylvia and her oven-baked hot dogs. She saved both Finn's and my life twice.

The night before I took Finn to get neutered at 15 months of age, we got into bed, and Finn came up to the head of the bed with me. He usually slept at or around my feet, at least to start. But that night, my boy came right up next to me, laid himself down alongside my head, and put his little front paw on my shoulder. Tears came to my eyes, and I couldn't help but think the worst. He always could sense when something was going to happen that he didn't want or like: when he would have to go to daycare, when he would have to get in the car (he was a puker), when I would pack my luggage for a trip. So it made me wonder if he "knew" something that I didn't.

I began to cry harder at the thought that he might not make it through surgery. I could not imagine my life without him. I was alone in the world, despite having amazing friends and love preservers. Those people all had their own tribes, and while I was part of their outer tribes, I was *the* priority for only Finnegan. Even when I was with Brennan, I was never the priority. On the totem pole of his priorities, I was a distant fourth...behind himself, Lorelei, and Clay. How I had longed to be someone's or something's first priority. Finally, I had found it in Finn. There was no greater love than this, and I knew that even if I were to find a man who truly loved me and put me first one day, the love of a dog was much like that of God.

It didn't take long for our bond to cement itself, perhaps two months. We both fell in love with the other, and nothing could ever break that bond, not even two trips that I had planned before Finn came home.

10

∿

Chapter 10: Salt Life, Part 1

Salt Life. One could find this phrase on bumper stickers, baseball caps, t-shirts, and the like. Salt Life was a popular brand of beachwear. But "salt life" took on many new meanings for me just after I moved back to Lancaster County.

First, a salt life to me meant "a new beginning and a separation from the past." In biblical times, salt was also used in purification processes. And I was in desperate need of all those things. I knew of no better way to accomplish those than to travel. I was anxious to get back to my wanderlust which had been shelved because of my anxiety and COVID. As a travel fiend, I had honed my skills on finding really great deals. By the end of 2022, I had established a strong superpower: I could travel like a rockstar on a dime.

Since I had four months of severance coming to me, and some time where I could do some healing—physically, mentally, spiritually—and it had been so long since I had taken a vacation to a destination of my choosing, I decided it was time to do so. And I decided that my first trip should be meaningful to me...should be therapeutic for me...should be inspiring to me. So I decided to go back to the land, the rocks, the desert that I visited the very first time I flew on an airplane in 1992...almost 30 years prior. And by mid-March, I had booked a trip to Sedona, Arizona. I found a hotel for one night, and an AirBnB for the remaining two nights, and made reservations for a few meals, as the end of April was part of peak tourist season. And found a good deal on a flight out of my tiny local airport, which was 12 minutes from door to door. Bam!

From the day after that I moved into my new apartment, I searched for a new job. I had had three interviews, but nothing quite worked out. I was looking for remote work, but I realized quickly I was competing with the entire country. That was a lot harder than competing with people within a 25-mile radius. When trip time rolled around, I was totally ready.

I secured up my Turo-rented pickup truck at the Sky Harbor Airport in Phoenix, and I headed out on the highways toward a little town called Jerome. The lead singer from the rock band Tool had a record store and winery storefront there. I got there with 15 minutes to spare before closing to pick up an autographed copy of his book for Brennan. Despite everything that had happened between us, I still cared about him immensely, and he was a huge Tool fan. I also bought a few LPs to start a vinyl collection for him.

Finally, I was off to dwell amongst the stunning red rocks of Sedona. They jutted out from the earth everywhere I looked, and each new view took my breath away. Finally, I could exhale. On the way to my hotel, I got distracted by a gem, crystal, and jewelry store. Once inside, I struck up a conversation with Rowen, a store clerk and Sedona local, who helped me pick a geode and pendant. And she also gave me a few suggestions regarding the energy vortexes I should visit based on what I wanted to achieve within myself. Jackpot!

After an OK night's sleep, I got up before dawn to go capture the sunrise over some red rocks. After researching some spots from which to see a good sunrise, I found one not far from my Hampton Inn on Hwy 89. I needed to get a little bit higher than I was at street level, so I wandered around til I saw a restaurant with a back deck. At 5:45 am, no one was at the place, but I still felt the need to sneak around the back and up the stairs. Mission accomplished! Photos captured. Potter County, PA claims to be "God's Country", but it had nothing on Sedona, AZ.

This first full day in Sedona was literally one of the best days of my life...seriously, top 5. Following a beautiful sunrise, I had the amazing fortune of meeting my new friend, massage therapist, fellow snorkeler, and spectacular human being. Thea introduced me to Jin Shin Jyutsu, the practice of releasing tensions in the body and harmonizing its life energy. And I felt like $10M when we were finished. There was no shortage of spas in Sedona, and I realized why I ended up at hers—it was exactly where I was supposed to be.

Thea confirmed that the vortex I should visit first was the little known and local secret called Buddha Beach in the middle of Oak Creek Canyon. So I set out to find it. I got a bit waylaid because—well, GPS. But as it turned out, it was also exactly where I was supposed to be. After an hour of hiking through the desert, not seeing another soul, I realized why Jesus wandered for 40 days there. It was peaceful...it was cleansing...it was clarifying...and it was beautiful. The desert was teeming with wildflowers, grasshoppers, mystery, cactus, and of course, whispers of truth. I eventually turned around as I realized I was not going to find Buddha's Beach on this path. On my way out, I met a family of six from Huntersville, NC. They helped provide some insight and showed me a map of where I should be looking for my desired destination. Little Hadley, age 4, and her 3-year-old brother, Logan, were enjoying their time with Grandma and Grandpa, and their smiles and spirits made me all the happier for my tiny detour.

I knew I was at the right spot when I had to pay $11 to enter, as Thea told me I would. I passed some stunning scenes on my way to the gorgeous, flat bedrock in the middle of Oak Creek Canyon. And I saw the spots Rowen told me about the night before. They were full of people picnicking, high school seniors skipping school, and some younger kids doing the same, I guess. But I couldn't blame them...I probably would have done the same on a gorgeous day like that one if I were a local. All I had to do was gingerly walk barefoot across some of the slippery, moss-covered rocks to a safe, dry one. I'm not as agile as I once was, and one wrong step could have meant cracking open my skull again, with nary a neurosurgeon in sight. But I pulled up my big girl panties and made it to the other side. I was in love with Buddha Beach! And it was more than I hoped for. I took pics of young people as they frolicked and fished and fell in love. And they returned the favor. Then I motioned to a 14-or-15-year-old boy to come over to me...because I was old, on the rock, and wasn't moving. He and a buddy had been kicking a volleyball like it was a soccer ball. So I asked him if he played soccer, and he said yes. Then I asked if he watched soccer on TV and who his team was. He said yes, and said that his international team was Columbia.

So I asked, "Cool...James, yes?" James is a Colombian footballer.

He smiled and said, "yes...Buenos Dias!" Then he said, "If we're talking Spanish League, then Barcelona!"

I smiled next, and said," Yes!!! But I miss Messi and Suarez so much!"

He was quick to add Neymar in the mix, and we both smiled at each other. I asked about the Premier League next, and he wasn't as into that, but asked if I was a Chelsea fan (my guess was because of American rockstar player, Christian Pulisic), and I said that my team was Tottenham. I also told him that I saw them play at Wembley in 2018.

He was impressed, and said he'd love to see Barcelona play. Eventually, he looked at me and said, "My name is John. What is your name?" So I told him, and he said, "It was so nice to meet you, Jordyn."

"Likewise, John," I returned with a smile. "Likewise." And I thought to myself, *What young, teenage boy stops to talk to a 49-year-old woman, and cares enough to ask her name?* The answer, it turned out, was John.

Having soaked in the views, people, and water on my personal slab of bedrock that my butt had claimed for an hour or so, I inched my way back to safety...with the help of two kind ladies on the shore who told me where to step. As I exited the water, I came across another family of six, from Henderson, NV. They were Filipino, and I spoke with the grandfather and grandmother quite a bit.

After a few minutes, the matriarch got a bit serious and asked me, "Are you traveling here from Pennsylvania all by yourself? No husband, no friend?"

And I replied, "Yes, I am by myself."

She grew more concerned, so I tried to reassure her.

"It's OK...I'm a big girl, and I'll be just fine." It didn't seem to make much difference to her furrowed brow. I smiled, said goodbye, and went on my way in search of a good spot to put on my shoes.

I found a tree stump, and the sweet grandpa had come along behind me and said, "What about that spot?" as he pointed to a stone bench about 50 yards away. Perfect. He came over to the bench with me, and we talked some more. We exchanged names...his was Ric. He wished me well on the rest of my trip, and I wished them a safe drive back to NV on Saturday.

Then he said, "It was nice to meet you, Jordyn...maybe we can meet up here again next year."

That would be lovely, Ric...truly lovely. And with that, we said our goodbyes, and I was off.

On my walk back to my truck, I realized I had learned a valuable lesson that morning: sometimes, the kindnesses of perfect strangers were more soul-touching, heart-warming, and Spirit-filled than how we are treated by family, by longtime friends, by people who "love" us...for one very special reason. The reason was because strangers took nothing for granted...they knew as well as I did that our meeting was not by chance, was not a coincidence, was not random...and they know that our paths may never cross again, and they make the most of our time together.

Tlaquepaque—the artsy village in Sedona that I had dreamed of going to for years—did not disappoint. I had a delish salad and my first libation of the trip—a yummy mule. Then I was off to shop. While walking through the village, I saw a little crystal/psychic reading shop. So again, when in Rome, I did that thing. I was asked to pick the person I wanted to do my 15-min reading from a binder with their pictures and bios. My first choice ended up not being available, so I made a second choice, Jeanie. As it turned out, she was no accident or coincidence either. She asked my birth month and day. As it turned out, she was born the same day! I'm not great at math, but even I could figure out the chances of that were 1 in 365. She rolled three dice and told me that my career needed to be both creative and spiritual in order to be fulfilling for me. Check and check. Then we did the cards. I shuffled and cut and shuffled again, then she flipped 11 of them. I won't go through it all, but it was awesome...good stuff coming work-wise, and also love-wise. I cried a little at one point at the not-so-randomness of what she was saying, and she offered me a tissue. It was good stuff, but heavy stuff. When we parted, she said she was going to say a prayer for me and one other...and I thanked her again.

When I got to my AirBnB for Thursday and Friday nights, I could not believe my fortune—the room, the bathroom, and the views from the driveway!!! But then I thought some more...of course this place was spectacular, why wouldn't it be?

I headed out to my dinner reservation, and as Spirit would have it, I was seated on the outside deck, right next to the railing and ginormous red rocks!!! And to my right were SueAnn and Jean, who took my photo, shared their story with me, and I shared mine for the fifth time in two days. They were on their honeymoon, even though they were already married two times, but still hadn't had their wedding (due to the CRUD). SueAnn's brother had had a stroke a few months ago and almost died due to a massive brain bleed. Once again...no random things in this world. This was God stuff. I enjoyed half of my dinner and decided to get dessert (a slice of pistachio cheesecake) to go, and I picked up a sweet red at the liquor store on my way back to the truck.

The end of the night...well, I ran a warm bath, placed a glass of the sweet red and the pistachio delight onto the metal tray that spanned the width of the tub. Yep, I indulged in a nightcap and dessert in a to-die-for tub!

The final lesson that day was that as much as I wanted someone to come with me on this trip, and I invited several, none of whom could go for various reasons, I **needed** to take this trip on my own. I **needed** to do exactly what I wanted to do, when I wanted to do it, and it had to be just me. And I was so happy I did.

I woke up at 2 a.m., a few hours later to look at the night sky, which was stunning. It was truly amazing what I could see without light pollution. Thousands and thousands of stars above my head in every direction. I felt so very small and so very loved at the same time.

My morning began a bit later than I wanted at Airport Mesa. And while I reached the summit a bit after sunrise, I still got to see some awesome sights, including three hot air balloons.

From there, I went back to Tlaquepaque, because I had to see the tiny chapel that I had wanted to be married in years ago. Since being married there was not meant to be, I decided on this trip that if I ever got married again, it would definitely be in this holy place. Even the little Striped Whiptail lizards know where to come to find Spirit, as one climbed on the head of a statue of a saint. I needed to know the names of the living creatures wherever I went. He had a beautiful blue belly that he would puff up and down. Daily visitors were not allowed in the chapel to avoid it being trashed every day. So I headed to the other holy spot I wanted to see.

The Chapel of the Holy Cross was built into the red rock, and was a stunning walk up a bit of a hill. Once at the entrance of the Catholic church, I quieted my spirit, and went inside. They had votives that people could light for a fee. The ones up front were three-day votives, meaning they were supposed to burn for three days before the acolytes put them out for someone else to light in honor of someone they wish God to bless, heal, and touch. I only had a $20 bill in my pocket, so I paid for four votives that would burn for three days and lit my candles. Then I began to cry as I prayed for health and healing for Brennan's cousin Seth, whose cancer has returned...for his uncle who had a recent cancer diagnosis and surgery...for his aunt, whom I loved very much and who bore the burden of having both her husband and son battling this evil...and for Grace, my friend and Seth's new wife with a few health issues of her own.

Hanging above the altar with votives was a crucifix like none I had ever seen, and it was mezmerizing. Jesus' eyes were wide open...like really wide. And the cross was actually a tree...and not just any old tree, but a fruit-bearing tree. I had to sit down for a few minutes to take that all in.

After my time in the Chapel, I chose a fun Mexican spot called Javelina Cantina for lunch. Javelinas are wild boars of the southwest, and the greeter said they even came onto the back deck sometimes. So of course I went out in search of them, but no luck. Then I hit the shops in the strip. One of the trinket stores was the Blue Lotus, where I met

Alisse, the 30-year-old shop owner, who made me green with envy of her job. She was a fun, colorful young woman who had two aquariums in her space. One held a large Koi named Kevin...and six other goldfish of a fancy variety, all named Kevin, Jr.

As we spoke about her fish, I told her she should refer to herself as Alisse, the mother of goldfish, "You know, like Daenerys," I said, a reference to the Game of Thrones mother of dragons.

And she replied, "Oh...I love that." And that's when I noticed the dragon tattoo on her forearm.

I said, "Tell me about your tat." And she giggled.

"Well, I gave myself this one night a few years ago after I drank too much tequila."

I wanted a bit more clarity around the arm artwork, so I said, "You mean someone gave you the tattoo when you were drunk?"

And she replied, "No...I gave it to myself."

I was stunned, looked at it more closely, and said, "Alisse...if that's what you can do when you are drunk on Tequila, I want to see what you can do sober!!!"

And she laughed and said, "I know, right?"

And although I was not a tequila drinker, I did know a few songs about the southwest liquor. So I said to her, "Hey, listen to this song...it's called 'Jose Cuervo' by old school country music artist Shelly West."

So she pulled it up on Spotify and played it over the store speakers. I'm not sure if Alisse was impressed that I knew all the words, or if she thought I was older than dirt. Later that night when I went back to the same plaza for dinner at another restaurant, I stopped in to tell her that I remembered the other song called "Tequila" by Dan+Shay. She thanked me and wrote it down.

As I kept walking through the plaza, I stumbled upon a sign for an art gallery that said "Franklin & Marshall College" on it! F&M was a private school in Lancaster, not far from my new place. So, I had to go and talk to the manager.

Mike, as it turns out, was a super interesting dude. His resume included a 21-year stint as a cop for the Department of Defense...so I of course had a bunch of questions for him, which he graciously answered —even the ones I thought he might shy away from.

At one point, Mike looked at me and said, "Jordyn, after 21 years in Government, most people are saying 'F—- you,' and happily walking away."

That was not at all what I was expecting. I thought for sure he would have been a Kool-Aid-soaked company man. Not so...and I even dipped my toe in the gun-control arena with this man from Texas (I know...what was I thinking, right?). But we actually agreed on the topic, and he schooled me a tiny bit about my own misinformation on what constituted a semi-automatic weapon. And I thanked him for that. Good dude...honest dude...informed and thoughtful dude.

And lastly...dinner. I had a reservation at a place called The Hudson. Gorgeous restaurant, and I was seated next to a table of six women who looked like they were on a low-key bachelorette trip. So I asked their waitress if that was the case, and if so, to please add a bottle of Prosecco to my bill for them to toast with. My waiter took the bottle to them, the bride-to-be, Lynelle, turned to me with a few tears in her eyes and lifted her glass to me, along with the rest of her table, and I in turn lifted my mule mug to them. After a bit, Lynelle came over to me and thanked me for my gesture. I asked if they were locals, and Lynelle said, "No, we're from Pittsburgh." And again, I was reminded that there were no coincidences...Pennsylvania girls! My heart had filled up. I told her I was from York County, but called Lancaster County home. And that I just moved from the suburbs of Philly.

She asked where in Philly, so I said "King of Prussia/Norristown area," and she said, "My sister and I grew up in Harleysville."

No way!!!! We hugged, and I enjoyed the rest of my meal and allowed them to do the same. At the end of my night, I walked over to wish her well once more, and when she asked if I had visited any vortexes, I happily shared Buddha Beach with them.

Another great day of connection with Spirit and new friends. It was holy, indeed.

On the third and final full day of my trip, I decided on the spur of the moment to hike through Soldiers Pass to the Devil's Kitchen—a huge sinkhole—and then the 7 Sacred Pools. It was fantastic and a true hike. I was huffing it a bit. But the views were totally worth it. And I met an adorable family on my way—Angela, Mike and their two sweet boys, Maximus (named after my favorite Gladiator) and Xavier. I also met Beatrice, Richard, and sweet German Shepherd boy, Hunter, from Kansas on my way back to the shuttle to the parking lot.

After the ridiculously crowded and HOT wine fest in Cottonwood, I made the easy drive back to Phoenix and found an awesome restaurant where I had delicious fondue and a sundae called the kitchen sink! A little more shopping was in order to kill some time before my red eye to Dulles. When I got to my gate at Phoenix airport, I met my new BFF Christina. She helped me zip up my carry-on, since I had to repackage to accommodate my new shopping treasures. Then we talked for the next 1.5 hours until our plane was ready to board. She was refreshing, agreeable, and so much my sister from another mister. My heart was still full up from the past four days.

Despite the fact that I had gone on this trip by myself, I was never, ever, ever lonely. I had talked to strangers...strangers who had become friends...strangers who had made connections with my heart and soul. And I was forever changed as a result of those interactions. And that was salt life—symbolic of a new beginning and a new hobby of talking to strangers because of the richness that each conversation brought to my life.

11

❧

Chapter 11: Salt Life, Part II

One short month later, I began another travel adventure with another love preserver whom I had known for decades. Vic and I began a friendship when we were in our late 20s after meeting at a new church plant, then we discovered we played volleyball on different teams but in the same league. We had lost touch for a bit while I was in the Philly suburbs, but reconnected on her 50th birthday over donuts and tea. So this trip to Turks & Caicos was her big event for the month of May. She decided to do something awesome each month of her 50th year of life, and I was more than happy to help out by asking her to join me in Provo (formally known as Providenciales), the most popular island in Turks & Caicos. Vic was one of the biggest beach lovers I had ever known, so she was the perfect travel companion to this destination.

I had been looking for airfare deals to anywhere, and one too good to pass up came along...and just like that, Vic was good to go! My traveling girl did not have any work or pleasure scheduling conflicts, so it was wheels up at the end of May!

Despite a few transportation snafus and a half-day delay, we eventually got on our plane and landed in what truly was paradise. Our first full day in Provo was nothing short of super cool...and there was no doubt why Grace Bay had just been voted the best beach in the world. It had

86

the softest sand, the most gorgeous water, and some pretty darn good snorkeling, despite being a popular destination. Popular beach locales with reefs typically were wrecked by beach goers who didn't know how to protect reefs by keeping their fins off the corals, not wearing reef-safe sunscreen, and just generally not paying attention to the delicate life below.

On Day 2, we took in all the beauty of Bight Beach, we chatted up Captain Marvin, who owned Marvin's Parasailing—the go-to for the likes of Drake, Jay-Z, Jeezy, Bill Clinton, and scores of other rich and famous personalities. We also got him talking about his time in the Middle East and the whale sharks he saw while diving Provo. It was my dream to swim with one...but Spike, the snorkeling boat dude who got us all fixed up for our boat tour on Wednesday morning, said he'd never seen one in T&C. So I decided to put that off til my 50th bday trip the following year.

We then moved down the beach a bit, had some lunch at Somewhere Cafe, and topped it off with a shared brownie sundae, before getting back into the water for our first snorkeling of the trip. Vic got to see a bunch of her firsts, including: a turtle, trumpetfish, blue tang, some new varieties of parrotfish, and sea fans. It was a good day below water...the salt water.

All that water time made me thirsty, so I bought a Coke for the beach. If our first two lunch bills did not make us realize we were on a pricey island, the $5 can of soda, plus $1 tip (volunteered) sealed the deal.

The main frustration of my day was my stupid flip flop. I kinda knew I shouldn't wear that pair, but I did anyway. The plastic thong between my big and second tootsies kept pulling out, which made walking through sand and on the macadam nothing short of exasperating...and I took to giving it several talking-tos as we made our 1/2-mile walk back to the car. Vic was fairly entertained...and super-entertained as I looked down after the 22nd time it came apart and proceeded to say out loud: "Look, it's not much farther...just get your life together, and when we get back home, you can have your final resting place in the circular file."

Then I looked up as Vic glanced at the construction dude across the street and said to him, "It's totally normal...just a girl talking to her flip flop...happens ALL the time, right?"

I mean, she could have given me a heads up...but nope. Then we both bent over laughing and howled like hyenas.

Next up was a quick trip to a convenience store because the IGA didn't have tiny containers of milk, which is all we needed for Vic's morning tea. So I stayed in the car, and when she returned, she plopped a Dove ice cream bar in my lap.

I looked at my watch then up at her and said, "Vic, you do remember we just had a brownie sundae 3.5 hours ago, right?" And with that, we both laughed again and proceeded to eat our treats. After all, we were PA Dutch girls to our very core, which meant we rarely met desserts we didn't like (save maybe German chocolate cake...because, gross).

We trekked over to the water sports shop to settle up with Spike for our boat snorkeling trip the next day, which was where we met Bella and Nicole—two 28-yr-old beauties who wandered into the shop. Bella, a stunner from Miami, was a self-proclaimed weak swimmer and wasn't sold on the trip, while the lovely Nicole from NYC was all set to try her fins at one of my favorite pastimes. So Vic and I went to work on them, and by the end of 15 minutes, they were signing on the dotted line and would join us on the boat the next morning at 9:00. We bid them adieu and did a little shopping...until I had to pee and stopped by a local, fancy-ish restaurant to use the facility. When I popped out, I heard "Joooorrrrrrdynnnn!" being yelled from across the atrium. Our two young recruits were at the bar having their first of many libations to come for the night. So we chatted again, invited them to a dinner one night this week, and once again parted ways til the morning.

I was worried about Wednesday, fearing the worst with these girls, who already told us we're doing shots on the boat...oy! I mean, it was a morning boat trip. I was prepared for the rum punch that was provided...and kinda looking forward to one or two as I headed down the sliding board off the boat and into that turquoise magic. But shots...and who knew what else? Well it was gonna be 5 o'clock in Ireland...we just happened to be in T&C. Oh well.

On Wednesday morning, Vic and I got up before dawn, packed our gear for the snorkel trip, and headed down to the Bight to watch the sunrise. It was magical, and not another soul on the beach. After we had more than enough sunrise photos, we sat a bit and waited for a little cafe called LMN to open. When we got there, we looked around at the quaint decor, ordered our teas, and sat down on a table outside. A handsome gentleman sat a few tables down from us, and in keeping with my new hobby of talking to strangers, I struck up a conversation with him.

Roger was a big shot real estate mogul with Christie's, I deduced from his branded white button down shirt. He and I must have spoken across the two empty tables between us for 30 minutes, and it was delightful, intelligent, and rather flattering. Before Vic and I headed out on our snorkel trip, we bid Roger goodbye, he flashed a big smile, and I reciprocated. Not a bad way to start the day, I thought.

Thursday's motto was one out of Nike's playbook. That day Vic and I "just did it." What was "it"? To be upfront about things..."it" wasn't "that." One of the things on Vic's 50th year list of "to dos" was to learn to sail, and so that day on Provo, Vic crossed another item off her checklist. I watched from shore, had a frozen beverage, and watched a pelican on a giant buoy.

As for me, I made an ask of Roger, the handsome realtor at the coffee shop yesterday. And while he wasn't able to help me with my ask that I made via text, which was for a job at Christie's in their marketing department, he did say we could have coffee again today. So I did it. And...after I kept him from his work for 1.5 hours Thursday morning, he invited me to come back on Friday for another chat.

Thursday night, we did the local things to do on the fourth night of each week, we went to the fish fry and live tunes at Danny Bouy's with our new girls, Bella and Nicole. We ate delicious fish, rice, and other island treats while drinking too many drinks, then hopping to another spot where I embarrassed myself on the dancefloor with my new young-thang friends. But it was totally worth the laughs...and possibly the videos. We dropped the girls off at their Club Med hotel, and we headed back to our AirBnb. Friday morning was coming soon, and I had a breakfast tea date with a former Brit-turned-islander.

Friday began like the last two days, with a chat over a cup of English

Breakfast at my fave cafe on Provo. Roger and I had some intense chats those three mornings, and when he had to head to his office after our third and final tête-a-tête, he stood up, leaned in, and hugged me. Whew! My head might have spun around for a minute. Then he reached into his wallet, pulled out a fancy business card, and asked for my phone. He laid it on top of my iPhone, and instantly, all of his contact information downloaded. Head spun around once more, and he smiled at my naïveté, graciously. Once more, he leaned in for a hug, I smiled and said I'd be in touch. And with that he was gone.

The trip to Turks & Caicos truly had been a gift in ways I could have never dreamed...and the main way was this: it had been as profoundly moving and spiritual as my trip to Sedona last month. Of course Provo was stunningly beautiful—with the softest sand my toes have ever stepped on, the most magnificent waters, and abundant sea life. But what I wasn't expecting were the beautiful, stunningly gorgeous, soulful (as in full of soul and spirit) people I met here. Just like Sedona, so many "chance" interactions, meetings, conversations that in reality we're not chance, not coincidence, not happenstance at all. From Canadian friends we made on the train platform in Newark, to our new sisters from other misters who were wise beyond their years and drop-dead gorgeous, to my cafe companion who taught me about soul contracts, among many other things—they were my reflections. Like Justin Timberlake sang in his song "Mirrors":

It's like you're my mirror
My mirror staring back at me
I couldn't get any bigger
With anyone else beside of me
And now it's clear as this promise
That we're making two reflections into one
'Cause it's like you're my mirror
My mirror, staring back at me, staring back at me.

As we left Provo after six full days, I thanked the island for the beauty it brought into my life that week. Then I thanked God for Provo, and for the richness, the sprinkles of seasoning that spiced up my week, for the friendship I had rekindled with Vic...for salt.

12

Chapter 12: 23 & (Are You Kidding?) Me

I'm with you and you're with me
We all are branches, branches on the family tree
It's in the blood all about the family
It's in the blood
It's in the blood all about the family.
—Londonbeat

In September of 2022, I decided to finally give in and get my DNA tested to confirm what I had grown up assuming was my heritage. I had decided not to do the test years before because I didn't not want the Government to be able to use any health findings against me for future insurance claims or the like. But when I realized that the Government could get whatever they wanted, whenever they wanted, for whatever reason they wanted, I reconciled with myself that it was more important to know where I came from.

When I received word on October 28, 2022 that my report was ready, I quickly flipped to the Ancestry Report part to find out if my lifelong suspicions were indeed correct.

Within seconds, I quickly deduced that my gut was indeed correct—my report showed that my heritage was 95.6% French and German, with my ancestors hailing from the Canton of Bern in Switzerland (the French part), and also coming from Bavaria (the German part). The remaining 4% had roots in Britain/Ireland/Scotland...with just a tiny sliver of a percentage that showed Viking. As I read more about these areas, I learned that the Canton of Bern was where many plain people came from—the Amish, Mennonites, Brethren, and several other smaller sects of Christians who fled their homeland due to religious persecution.

And those Swiss/German ancestors were almost certainly what's known as Old Order Mennonites...and definitely anabaptists. None of my grandparents or great-grandparents were anabaptists, but it was surely in my blood, based on what the report showed. And one month prior to reading this report, I had been rebaptized...this time into the Brethren in Christ tradition, an Anabaptist (which means "baptized again") tradition.

This got me thinking about the things, the people, the lands I had been attracted to in my life. The two longest relationships I had had with men were with Irish and Scotch-Irish men. The puppy that I chose to be my first fur baby had ancestors hailing from Scotland. Granted, these were very, very small parts of my makeup, but they were still there. And the English bits of me? Well, my love of Premier League soccer had that covered in spades. Football was one of the loves that was ignited by Brennan, and I found it was something that I didn't want to give up. Maybe it was something that I couldn't give up...because it was part of me. The modern game hailed from London around 1863, and my team (Tottenham) also called North London home.

Then there was my affinity for all things France. I studied French for six years, and to my French professor's dismay, I did not double major in French and English, or even minor in French...but man, I wish I had. I fell in love with Paris when I visited for the first time in 2018. And I felt so much at home in the City of Light, despite being a country girl...like part of me was meant to be surrounded by French culture, people, art, and life.

And that Viking part...well, as it happened, one of my volunteer jobs in the spring of 2022 was for an axe-throwing meadery with Viking roots in Lancaster. I traded my marketing expertise for the opportunity to throw axes whenever I wanted. And I became enthralled with Netflix series like *Vikings Vahalla* and *Ragnarok*. Perhaps my DNA dictated that attraction as well.

So, no...my report was not kidding me. It told me everything that I never knew I needed to know. And it was spot on. Sometimes knowing where one comes from helps her to know where she should be going.

13

～

Chapter 13: Salt Life, Part III

In February 2023, I began a new chapter of my life...I entered my sixth decade on Planet Earth. And it had been a long-time dream to spend it in style and in a bucket-list destination. So despite not having full-time work at the time, I seriously began looking at the travel emails that fluttered into my email boxes each day, and one day in March 2022, I saw a fantastic deal on a trip to the Maldives—one of my top of the list spots to spend a dream vacation. I knew very few people would have the time or money to go with me, except for perhaps Brennan. So, I asked him, because for a few years, we had discussed our 50th birthdays and where we might want to spend them. Interestingly, he said "yes." So, I booked the trip, Brennan sent money for his portion of the trip via Venmo, and I put it all on my credit card. I used airline miles to book my ticket for free, and I agreed to split his ticket with him, as that seemed fair to me.

Brennan and I had had more than our fair share of fights in the 11 months leading up to the trip...some of which meant canceling smaller road trips we had planned in between booking the Maldives trip and taking the Maldives trip. We were not back together, but we had tried to be friends and traveling/concert companions after the demise of our relationship. So we got on a plane that left Philadelphia for Doha, and away we went. We spent 14 hours in the air to reach Doha in Qatar. The

95

next seven hours were in the airport, followed by another 4.5-hour flight to Male, the capital of the Maldives. After another three-hour layover in Male, we took a 50-seat airplane on a one-hour flight to our little island. We had logged 30-ish hours of travel door to door, but we made it. I was in paradise. I was with my ex-partner, but I was there!

And, oh my! It was everything I had dreamed of, except for the whale sharks. I had wanted to swim with the whale sharks on my 40th birthday in Turks & Caicos, but I had filed for divorce from my ex-husband before that happened. So when I began dreaming about my 50th birthday trip, I came back to the whale shark idea. These gentle, plankton-eating giants were so docile and beautiful, and I was so excited to be in the water with one or more of them. But those dreams came crashing down when I learned that our island was too far south to see whale sharks. So I would have to wait for a different trip to see them.

The reality was: I was in paradise, in an over-the-water villa, with snorkeling right off the back deck any time I wanted it, and there was a hole in the floor of the villa with a glass pane covering it so that I could watch the fish right below us anytime I wanted.

When we arrived at the resort around 1:30 in the afternoon, our room was not quite ready. So I grabbed a swimsuit from my backpack, found a beachside restroom in which to change, and hit the main pool in front of Helene, the main restaurant. I was in heaven, staring out across the horizon, dotted with villas...and one of them was mine for the next nine nights. I almost could not believe my eyes, I mean I know I put a small fortune on my credit card to be there, but it really did feel like a fairytale...**my** fairytale that came true!

When the concierge drove us, courtesy of a golf cart, to our villa, we found a lovely yet compact room with a complimentary stocked minibar, bottled water, and a drawer filled with snacks, all of which were restocked daily. The bathroom was gorgeous with a double vanity, large soaking tub, and an indoor shower. Just beyond a glass door, we found an enclosed outdoor shower. Our deck overlooked the stunning blue waters of the Indian Ocean as well as our private infinity pool. This was absolutely the most opulent trip I had ever taken...and after all I had endured in the past few years, a part of me felt I was justified in taking this trip. In taking any and all trips. Something inexplicable happens when you wake up from surgery to find out that you almost died not once, but twice. You don't take a single thing for granted anymore...including the very breaths you draw. And while trips to foreign countries may seem wasteful, irresponsible, or just decadent to many with a scarcity mindset, that has never been my view. And even though I did not have a full-time job, I knew that getting full-time work was just a matter of time. But I had also learned that I never really knew when my last grain of sand will fall through the hourglass of time. And so, here I was...ready to embrace ten days of spectacular views, sunrises, sunsets, snorkeling, all-inclusive eating and drinking (yes, even the fully-leaded stuff), and water sports.

And all of those things were absolutely fantastic, but the truly amazing stuff revolved around people. I met a young, newly-wedded couple from Australia who played cards with me at a cocktail hour while we discussed socialized medicine. I met a lovely couple from France, with whom I practiced my French. I met an American couple who now lived in Canada...and the husband and I bonded over our mutual Tottenham Hotspur fandom. He also told us how to attempt to watch the Super Bowl on our TV.

But my most meaningful, powerful conversations occurred with two of the staff members at the Maldivian resort. I met Smith, a 22-year-old expat from India, at the second restaurant at the resort. Smith worked hard as a server in both restaurants, and I knew when I saw him that there was something special about him. He had kind, honest eyes, an authentic smile, and a genuine interest in providing exceptional service to all guests.

My very first question to Smith was, "Your name tag says 'Smith,' but that is your last name, right?"

He smiled and replied, "No, my first name is 'Smith'."

I looked puzzled, and he saw that on my face.

"My last name is my father's first name," he continued. "And Smith is my first name."

"Oh, OK," I replied. "Can I ask you another question, Smith?"

He nodded and smiled.

"How many people treat you and the other wait staff badly?" I asked next.

Smith smiled and leaned a bit closer as he said, "Not very many at all, really. Maybe one in 100 people. And that one has not earned his own money. He does not know what hard work is."

I smiled back and nodded in acknowledgment and a bit of surprise that such a young man was so astute, so intune with the nature of those around him.

We saw Smith later that night when we went back to shoot pool upstairs. We talked soccer with him and the bartender until we closed the place down a few minutes after 11 p.m.

I would learn just how amazing the service at the resort was on my 50th birthday. After finding the Super Bowl on the regular TV stations, minus the U.S. commercials, we went for breakfast, puttered around the villa, caught some rays, and I did the Nestea plunge in our private, little infinity pool. After lunch, we returned to find that housekeeping had not only cleaned our room, but also left a gorgeous message on the bedspread for me. In palm leaves, they had written 'Happy 50th Birthday,' had folded towels into a heart and a bunny pillar. The staff had strewn hibiscus petals all over the bedspread. Needless to say, I was so stunned...so thrilled...so surprised.

We did a nice snorkel trip off the back of the villa, and I showered up for a spa treat, and I had booked for myself. They had a great deal on a two-hour package that included a massage, a facial, and a cocoa body scrub, so I booked it.

At 3:45 p.m., I made my way across the walkway and through the forest to the spa. It was here that I had my second powerful encounter with a staff member of the resort. Thiny delivered my spa treatment in the afternoon. She was the slightest of women, a dark-haired, lovely, 28-year-old from Bali. She was so small and petite that I wondered how she could possibly give deep-tissue massages. I was not a fan of those, but I knew others were. However, Thiny was a well-trained, thorough, consummate professional who was capable of very, very hard work.

For the next two hours, we talked about our lives, almost without pause. I shared about my brain surgery, my job loss, my breakup with Brennan, my move back to Lancaster. And Thiny spoke of her life in Bali with her family—Mom, Dad, one brother, and two sisters. She spoke of how difficult life was during COVID, and how she struggled hard to make any money at all during that time. And perhaps an hour and a half into my treatment, Thiny asked me a question I will never forget.

"Jordyn," she briefly paused. "Have you ever been poor in your life? Like, really poor?"

After a second, during which I thought about the fact that I had not been gainfully employed in more than a year and was dipping into my last 401k to survive, I replied, "No, no I haven't."

Because after all, I was lying on a massage table in the Maldives at an all-inclusive resort and staying in an over-the-water villa. And although I had considered canceling this trip because I was still not employed after a year, my friends convinced me to go. Despite all these things, I knew I was filthy rich by comparison to my newest friend.

"You know, Jordyn," Thiny continued. "We do not get to eat the same food as you do in the restaurant. We eat at the canteen. And the food is not good. It is why I lost so much weight. So my dream is to save up enough money to buy a breakfast at Helene."

"How much would it cost you to eat breakfast, Thiny?" I asked.

"Thirty US dollars," she responded.

"OK," I nodded. I had just learned that she made $500/month, most of which she sent back to her family in Bali. When broken down per hour, she earned less than $2.25. In theory, she would make more with tips. But Thiny told me that many guests assumed that because they were at an "all-inclusive" resort, that meant tips as well. Ugh. And if they did tip, it was a dollar to two...but that was not often.

When Thiny had finished my luxurious treatment, she asked me to take my time getting up, but to make my way to the enclosed outdoor shower to get all of the cocoa scrub off me. I enjoyed my time in the shower, thinking back on the enlightening conversation I had just had with my friend, Thiny. When I finished, I put on my dress for the night and came out refreshed and relaxed.

Thiny came back with a glass of ginger-infused water for me and escorted me back to the front desk area. She asked me to sit down, disappeared for a moment, and re-emerged with a bouquet of flowers, wrapped at the bottom with palm leaves. She also presented me with a big palm leaf that had "Happy Bday, Jordyn...Love, Spa" spelled out on it.

I had never been more spoiled, ever, on my birthday...or any day. My heart was so full, I thought it might explode.

"Thank you so much," I said to Thiny and the spa manager. "You've made my birthday so special!" Then I signed the receipt for the spa treatment, and I tipped my new friend $30.

Thiny hugged me, and we exchanged WhatsApp and Instagram information so that we could keep in touch. I had already planned to come back the next day, which happened to be Valentine's Day, with the chocolate bar from our mini bar. Thiny had said how much she enjoyed chocolate during our two hours together, so I thought she would enjoy that.

Brennan was also surprised about my gifts from the spa and commented about how thoughtful it was, since I had never mentioned it was my birthday. The staff, apparently, got a list of important days in each guest's life while on the island. I walked on Cloud 9 the rest of the night. We walked over to the seafood buffet that night, sat outside to enjoy the breeze and sounds of the ocean. It was a nice way to end the night. Except that it wasn't quite over.

At 8:40 p.m., I headed back to our villa to prepare for a virtual job interview. I had been contacted by a recruiter on the day we left for the trip. I had not applied for this job, but the HR recruiter had found my information on LinkedIn. Since she was certain the hiring manager would want to meet me sooner than later, we found a time that worked for both of us...which happened to be at 9 p.m. on my birthday. It went super well, and he told me at the end of the interview that he would like me to come in to meet the team when I returned. Ya-hoo! It really was the perfect birthday! And I was so glad I had decided to take this trip, because it seemed like I might have had a real shot at a job when I returned home.

The next day, I saw Smith in Helene. I motioned for him to come over.

"I have another question for you," I began. "There is so much food left over at each meal, what happens to it?" Hunger and homelessness have been hot button issues for me since I had worked in center city Philadelphia from 2014-2016. I had seen way too much of both. And I gave whatever I had, whenever I could. So I was eager to know what happened to all the good food that was not eaten by guests.

"It gets thrown out," Smith said. He saw my face drop...and then get angry.

"What?!" I asked incredulously. "That makes me so mad! The staff does not get to eat the leftover food?"

"No," he said quietly. "Food service staff do get some of the leftovers, but not the other staff," he added.

I shook my head again. "Wait...there is no good reason not to share that food with all the resort staff," I replied. "Why throw food away when the staff could enjoy it...instead of lesser-quality food in the canteen?"

Smith simply smiled as best he could, because, as I gleaned from the look on his face, he thought the same thing.

I dropped off a chocolate bar to Thiny that day, as well as the next few days. On Friday, the day before we were leaving to go home, I stopped by the spa and invited Thiny to be my guest for breakfast on Saturday. She happily accepted.

"Oh, Jordyn!" she exclaimed. "That would be so nice!"

We settled on 8:30 a.m., and I met her at Helene the next morning.

"Hi, Thiny!" I greeted her with a hug.

"Good morning, Jordyn!" Thiny squealed. "I am so excited!"

I asked her to choose a table, and we began filling our plates.

Smith came around to take our drink orders, and I took the opportunity to ask him to take a few pictures of Thiny and me. He graciously obliged. Then we continued eating. Thiny constantly commented on how good everything was.

"Jordyn, aren't you going to eat more than that?" Thiny asked as she examined my plate with one scoop of scrambled eggs, one biscuit, and a few chunks of fruit. "I can get those eggs in the canteen," she continued. "But never an omelet! And the potatoes...and the fruit!" she exclaimed.

"Wait!" I started. "You can't get fruit in the canteen?" I asked.

"We get fruit, but not like this!" Thiny replied, examining the gorgeous papaya and melon on her plate. "Never this fresh and never this good."

Again, I found my blood pressure going up. What on Earth would make executives somewhere in charge of this resort think that the staff deserved anything less than the same quality food that we received? Were they less human than paying guests? Did they do something to deserve a lesser quality food? No. No. No...they had not. In fact, they had provided the best service of any hotel or resort I had ever patronized. Yes, it was true that they received lodging for free. But that, too, was less than ideal. Six women to three sets of bunk beds in one room. No privacy, no room of one's own. Same for the men.

Smith received $17/day, six days a week. Any tips that the bartenders received were split with the servers, too. But again, many guests never tipped bartenders, under the same premise that it was an all-inclusive.

After breakfast, we took a few more pictures, and I wished her well, promising to keep in touch. I told Smith I would see him later.

At 7 p.m. that night, we were supposed to get picked up for a golf cart ride to the airport, about a half-mile away. I looked high and low for Smith, but I could not find him to say goodbye. Thiny had stopped by Helene and surprised me with a pair of beautiful gold earrings from Bali. We hugged again, said our goodbyes, and Brennan and I were on our way to the airport.

I had no idea that the two sweet, young friends I had made during my stay in the Maldives would end up being another salt story. This time, the salt aspect that began on our little island in the Indian Ocean and continued each day since my return home via WhatsApp centered around the idea that salt represents a long-lasting relationship, a friendship, and God's never-ending love for us.

Smith, Thiny, and I have texted or video called over WhatsApp every day since I left the Maldives. In that time, we have forged such bonds, that Smith, his girlfriend, and Thiny all plan to come to the U.S. on work visas in the near future, with the intent of sharing a home with me, which will be called the Salt Preserve.

The Salt Preserve will represent a place of sanctuary, refuge, and diversity among friends who will protect, love, and care for each other. And it will be filled with salt-of-the-earth people.

14

Chapter 14: I Knelt to Refill My Vessel, But I Was Shoved in the River

That interview that I had on my 50th birthday in the Maldives landed me an interview three days after my return to the States. I met with two people in person, and three virtually. Each conversation went super well, including the last conversation with the HR recruiter, Amy.

"So, Jordyn," Amy began. "If you were hypothetically to be offered this position, what is your current situation? That is, do you have other offers pending, other interviews?"

"Actually, I do," I replied. "I am expecting to hear about another offer soon."

She went on to tell me about the benefits, the PTO, the hybrid work environment, and the culture.

"Ok, we will likely make a decision by Friday," she said. "Middle of next week at the very latest."

"Sounds good," I said. "I will wait to hear from you." And with that, I shook her hand and went on my way. I sent thank you emails to everyone as soon as I returned home.

I was just hoping that they called me before the other offer, since that one was only part-time with a much lower hourly rate.

I got the call at 2 p.m. that day from the other company, offering me the part-time role. I asked when they needed an answer from me. The HR director said that by Friday would be great. I thanked her, saying I would be in touch soon.

Crap.

I called Brennan and talked over a strategy for this with him. We both agreed that if I didn't hear from the FT gig that I really wanted by Friday at noon, I would call to see if any decision had been made.

While impatiently waiting, I received a call on Friday at 10 a.m., and I was offered the job. To say I was thrilled was a massive understatement! I accepted on the spot, and I proceeded to tell her how I was going to call at noon, since I had received another offer on Wednesday.

"Oh, I'm so glad I called when I did," Amy began. "Andre would have been so upset to have lost you! He has been talking about you ever since your interview with him while you were in the Maldives!"

"Seriously?" I asked in almost disbelief. I mean, it had been over a year since I was gainfully employed full-time.

"Absolutely," Amy confirmed. "He kept asking me this week if I had called to offer you the role. He knew you wouldn't last long...that someone else would snatch up someone with your skill set."

It was all I could do not to laugh right out loud! If she/they only knew how many places had turned me down, had strung me along, had said how amazing I was and that I would get a second interview...only to be ghosted or told the job went to someone else, how many times I was told, "Thanks for interviewing with us, while you were qualified, we decided to select another candidate..." only to see the job reposted the very same day.

I had been through the ringer when it came to finding another job, and when I would share my tale of woe with other women friends, I heard nothing but resounding affirmations of the same. The general consensus was that ageism was alive and well in the greatest country in the world, especially for women of a certain age...and that age happened to be 50.

I was absolutely dumbfounded each time I was passed over, despite having great interviews, despite answering questions with clarity and confidence, despite my more than two and a half decades of applicable experience. I just didn't get it. I kept asking myself why I was repeatedly being passed over for roles I was more than qualified for...coordinator roles, specialist roles, manager roles. After all, I had held titles of "Sr. Manager" and "Director" before. Certainly I could handle a role that was several degrees less advanced.

Beyond that, I began to notice another pattern that was almost just as disturbing to me: the fact that most of these hiring managers were women in their early- to mid-30s. Where was the "girl power"? Where was the sisterhood? Where was the support for one another in a man's world? I was completely disillusioned. And so, again, I took to speaking with other women friends. Unfortunately, they had confirmed my experiences, saying that Millennial women, generally speaking, were not interested in hiring someone older than them...someone who might be able to teach them something...someone who might know something they didn't. In short, there was an intimidation factor that they had a hard time getting past.

I had begun to lose hope that I would ever find another good job again. I was ready to resign myself to the pasture beyond my apartment, because that was what I saw in my future–being put out to pasture. So much for a resume with plenty of valuable, solid experience...no one wanted that. They wanted to hire their friends...or at least people their own age.

But then, in the knick of time, Amy and Andre entered the picture with an offer, accompanied with a professed strong workplace culture and the best salary I had ever earned. It was so hard to believe that my job drought was finally over! In six working days, I would be earning a good wage again! I could begin paying down the credit card debt I had incurred over the past year, begin building my depleted 401k back up again, and begin saving for a house for Smith, Thiny, and me. This was my answer to prayer after prayer after prayer.

"Thank you, God!!!" I said this repeatedly on more than one occasion. I knew where my help came from.

The first two days were almost perfect. I had settled into my cubicle, put out all my books, decorations, and filled up my drawers with supplies. At the end of Day 2, I was instructed by Andre to meet with a new teammate who was being moved from the production department to marketing...my department. Aiden was great. We were like two peas in a pod. We spoke for more than two hours about the company, what he had observed in his short nine weeks on the job, and that what was professed about the corporate culture might not be exactly the way it was. Aiden let more than a little air out of my balloon with his observations, but I was still holding out hope for a good workplace.

On Day 3, things started to go downhill. There was an issue with business cards, which I had just taken over. I had done everything just as Andre had requested, but a request was made of me that he had said absolutely "no" to originally. On Day 4, he asked HR to call a meeting with him, me, and HR. It was under the guise of just checking in to see how things were going, but in my gut, I knew there was something more to it than a check-in.

At any rate, I said that everything was fine from my perspective, and that I was learning how everyone preferred to be communicated with. Andre was from South America, so English was his second language, and I sometimes needed to ask him to repeat himself.

At the end of the day, I ran into Amy in the break room. I asked her about the meeting we had had.

"Hey, Amy," I said, "was today's meeting your idea, or did Andre ask you to call it?"

"Oh, it was my idea," she quickly said.

"Really?" I asked. "He seemed upset with me yesterday, simply because I copied both you and Rose on the business card emails."

Amy assured me over and over and over again that everything was fine...that I was simply overthinking things.

Day 5 was a work-from-home day, and Andre called me on MS Teams, but not on a video call, which I didn't really understand. It was two full hours long. I tried to ask questions as he quickly rattled off information, while I took furious notes. But he simply talked louder and over top of me.

"Andre, Andre, can I please talk? Just for a minute? Then you can talk again?" I begged. Eventually, he gave me the 30 seconds I needed to detail what I wasn't understanding.

"Jordyn!" he screamed. "I am being SO clear here! I am being SO clear!!!"

Not wishing to point out the obvious, I just took deep breaths and let him go on. The call eventually ended, and I finished out my day by going downtown at 5:30 p.m. on a rainy, Friday night to hand off newly printed emergency business cards to a new coworker who had to get on a plane on Sunday morning for a tradeshow on Monday, where he would be giving out his contact info all day long. The last two sets of cards, which Andre had printed, both had wrong information on them, which is why Christian contacted me. I fixed the error, had Staples print them in a rush order, and Christian was good to go!

On Friday night, I coordinated with my high school bestie, her boyfriend, and his work wife to book an amazing deal of a trip to Italy in November 2023. Finally! I could travel guilt-free again. I was making good money, so when great travel opportunities arose, I could jump on them without worrying how I was going to pay for them. By 10:30 p.m. on Friday night, we were all set for wheels up in October. I was beyond thrilled. I never thought I'd be able to go to Italy for that kind of price...in my lifetime!

Monday morning rolled back around, and Andre and I were both working from home again. I sent him a *"good morning...hope you had a good weekend"* message over MS Teams around 7 a.m. He wasn't online yet. So I began working on a piece of collateral for Christian. He eventually responded with "good morning" somewhere around 8:45. I heard nothing more from him until 1:20 p.m., when I was on my lunch hour and happened to be at the bank, trying to resolve an issue. I had put my "unavailable" status on my Teams account, like he had asked me to do last week. But I responded anyway.

"I'm at the bank right now, trying to resolve an issue with my account. Can we meet at 2:00?" my message back to him said.

"Yes, that is fine" was his reply.

I returned to my home at 1:40, exactly one hour after I left to go to the bank. At 2 p.m., he called me.

"Hello, Andre," I said.

"Jordyn, when you are going to be away like that, you need to let me know," Andre came at me.

"Huh...what?" I questioned. "I was on my lunch hour."

"Yes, but if you are going to be gone for an extended period of time, I need to know about it," he retorted.

"But I was not gone for an extended period of time," I assured him. "I left at 12:40, and I returned at 1:40."

"Yes, but if you are going to be doing something like that, I should know," he was not giving in.

"Wait," I said. "You need to know where I go and what I do during my lunch hour?"

"THAT! That right there, Jordyn!" he blasted back. "That tone is what I'm talking about. I AM YOUR SUPERIOR!"

I took a quick and disbelieving breath. But he continued with a vengeance.

"This is not working for me. I'm calling HR right now."

And those were the last words I ever heard him say. And Day 6, was the last day of my employment with that company...a company that was very clearly talking a desired walk regarding culture, but not walking it.

Two days later, at 5:30 p.m., I met Amy and her boss, Christine, in the vestibule of my former workplace. I went in to collect my belongings...only to find that they had been collected for me. We weren't off to a good start. What on Earth could have been the harm in allowing me the opportunity to make sure everything that was mine was out of my cubicle and desk?

"First, let me say that I'm sorry, Jordyn," Christine said. Amy nodded in agreement.

"This is not the outcome we had hoped for, Jordyn," Amy said with her gaze dropping to her lap.

"Yeah, that makes three of us," I responded.

"Is everything in the box?" Christine asked.

"I have no idea," I replied. "I was not afforded the opportunity to go through my desk." I took a quick look through the box. "My books are not in here!" I said rather heatedly.

"Where are they?" Christine asked.

"On top of my desk." I was so freaking annoyed. I mean, seriously. Did they think I was going to take the stapler? If I had thought of it at the time, I would have said that I'm only interested in red Swinglines, but I'm pretty sure that iconic pop culture reference would have been lost on her.

While Christine was gone, Amy, a young mid-20-something fire-cracker, took the time to apologize several times to me. "I'm so sorry, Jordyn. I'm so sorry about all this."

"Yeah. Me, too," I whispered, barely acknowledging her with a side eye as I eked out the words. "If you recall, I could have taken the other job." I had to add a little insult to the injury. After all, it seemed fair. She recruited me to work for a man with a superhuman ego, but with insecurities of the same magnitude, apparently. I knew she was only doing the job she was hired to do...to find and hire other people. But I wanted her to know that she should not actively recruit again for this position. So when Christine returned with my books, I gave them a few pieces of advice.

"Oh, this book," I said as I held up the cover for them to see, "this book is one Andre should read." The book was titled "Thanks for the Feedback." Then I looked up and asked, "May I?" essentially asking if I could speak.

Christine nodded and motioned for me to begin.

"Do not hire a woman for this role," I directly and purposefully said. And with that, Christine took out her pen and paper and began taking notes. I was remotely impressed. I did not elaborate. As I scanned both of their faces, it was clear that I did not need to expound. They implicitly understood.

"Also, do not recruit for this role," I continued, then looking at Amy. "If someone takes this role, let it be because they found the job req on-line and thought they'd be a good fit...not because you sought them out, promised them a bed of roses, and then dumped 16 shovelfuls of manure on top of the seeds."

Amy's head dropped. Message received; mission accomplished.

"Jordyn, I am so sorry," now it was Christine's turn. "I'm sorry it worked out this way."

I had never heard of a firing where there were so many apologies from the people doing the firing. It really was almost surreal. I nodded once more. That was enough. There was nothing left to say, except, well...maybe.

"In the grand scheme of things, this is a big fat NOTHING," I began. "You see, I cheated death twice in 2021 on an operating table. My neurosurgeon called me his 'miracle baby,' so truly, this is NA-THING!!! Nothing at all."

I was **finished**. They sat there in silence, glancing back and forth at one another, as I picked up my banker's box full of desk items, and walked out the door. I got into my car, hit the ignition button, and backed out. When I got to the stop sign. I paused. This was really happening. I had what I thought was the perfect job, with the perfect amount of pay, with what I thought were the perfect coworkers...only to find that "perfect" does not exist...anywhere.

# # # # #

Square One! There you are, my old friend. I thought you had gone on vacation...and maybe you had. Guess it was only for six days. Certainly, not long enough. Vacations are never long enough, are they?

15

Chapter 15: Siren Wails, Storm Revisited, and Saying Goodbye

"The secret of life is knowing when to leave." –Danny Rayburn, *Bloodline*

Brennan and I had hung out two times after returning from the Maldives, but that came to an abrupt halt when I learned that he had used Lorelei's new husband, James, as his realtor. I could not believe my eyes when I saw James' website that included Brennan's new home on it. Yes, for reasons I just could not fathom nor understand, Brennan chose James, over thousands of other realtors in Montgomery County to give his $4,000 in realtor fees to. In my mind, this had Lorelei written all over it. There was no end to the amount of money she would try to take from Brennan's bank account...and she successfully talked her way into another $4,000. Well played, Siren...well played. But I was less than impressed. In fact, I was more than over her money-grubbing, con-jobbing ways.

Brennan and I had another blow up over this decision to willingly hand her more money that she didn't need. I was sure this was all under the guise of convenience and "knowing James." Brennan rebuked me.

Brennan: Jordyn, this has nothing
to do with you.

> Me: Yes, I'm sure you see it that
> way. Along with all the other decisions
> you've made regarding her and Clay
> over the years that had unfortunate side
> effects for me. Did she need a new pair
> of shoes, Brennan? I mean, she already
> has two brand new houses and a Jaguar.
> On the other hand, I am three months
> away from being homeless, but you in-
> sist on lining her already FAT wallet.

Brennan: You are so misinformed,
Jordyn. It was convenient to use
James, and I used him as a thank
you for paying for Clay's health
insurance.

I laughed out loud when I read that. James was a civil servant, and Clay's healthcare insurance cost $2/month. Brennan could have written him a check for the two year's worth of insurance that totaled about $50, and it would have been a lot cheaper, and so much less offensive to the person he spent the last eight years of his life with...the person he had called his best friend.

Why did it always come back to her? Why? She left a path of destruction at every corner of his life and Clay's, and yet, he just seemed not to be able to cut her out of his life. And so if he couldn't, wouldn't cut her out, I had no choice but to cut him out of my life. Because I was no longer willing to be tethered to anything that wouldn't let me fly into the future that awaited me. My time of suffering because of her had come to an end.

So, six days before Brennan's birthday, I sent him a text wishing him a happy birthday, saying this would be the first birthday of his in a decade where I would not be celebrating him. And that that made me very, very sad, but that it was what I needed to do. He thanked me.

On the day before his birthday, I sent one more message to him.

> Me: Goodbye. Always remember that I loved you better than anyone, but it just wasn't enough.

A few minutes later, I got a reply.

Brennan: What's 'goodbye' supposed
to mean?

I did not answer.

About 30 minutes later, he tried calling me. I did not pick up. Another message appeared after the unsuccessful call.

Brennan: Tried calling. Please
don't do anything rash.

Again, I did not reply. And about 20 minutes later, my sister called me. I knew when her name showed up on my phone that Brennan had reached out to her. I picked up the call.

"I'm guessing that Brennan texted or called you," I said after exchanging pleasantries.

"Yes," said Stacy. "What's going on?"

So I began filling her in on the latest, and on how I just could not stand any more of Lorelei's steaming piles. Stacy didn't quite understand why I had to cut off things completely with Brennan, but it just felt like the only way for me to heal and move on.

When the day before his birthday arrived, I fired up a Zoom call with five dear friends who were wholehearted supporters of my finally moving on. So, I had read a little diatribe that I had written, and each of them patiently listened as I poured out my hurting heart once more.

And then I took three little slips of paper out and held them up to my laptop camera for all to see. One had the word "blame" written on it, one had the word "shame", and the last one had the word "flame." Next, I held up a tiny little plastic brown flower pot with some potting soil in it. And very ceremoniously, I deliberately buried each of those words one at a time.

I decided to stop placing all of the blame for my circumstances at his feet. I had made some poor financial decisions that contributed to my situation as well. So no more blaming. I also decided to stop shaming myself for not respecting myself from the beginning...for tolerating what appeared to be his choosing Lorelei over me time and time and time again. And finally, I buried the flame that I had carried for Brennan for a decade. I would never, ever find true love if I continued to pine for a man who just wasn't capable of loving me. And with that, I released myself from the hold that Brennan had had over me and my life. And I had released him as well...to go and live however he chose. I closed with a prayer, mostly thanking God for receiving me back into his open arms, despite my poor choices.

My girlfriends supported every aspect of the ceremonial breaking free session. They said lovely and kind things to and about me. And then, we all turned off our Zoom screens, and I was left to step out on my own.

And I did. For two whole weeks. It was the longest I had ever gone without any form of communication with Brennan.

And then...

16

❧

Chapter 16: He Just Seemed So Sweet

#Metoo.

17

Chapter 17: Not Invited...But Welcomed to an Extent

(trigger warning)

Two weeks to the day that I had written off Brennan "for good," I had gone on a date. We met out for a light meal. Light...mainly because he was cheap. The number of first dates I had been on where a man actually paid for the meal could have been counted on one hand. And while he had paid, we shared an eight-inch pizza.

Then he wanted to come back to my place for ice cream. I was hoping we would continue to talk and get to know one another. I was hoping we would do what Brennan and I did for 1.5 years, which was sit and talk across the room from one another...about religion, about current events, about politics, about music and movies and literature. But it was not to be.

# # # # #

Eight hours later, I sent Brennan a text message.

> Me: I dreamt that you came for me last night...that you rescued me. That somehow, you just knew that I needed you. And indeed I did. But in reality, you didn't come, of course. I never should have had to endure what I did last night. Perhaps I will simply swear off men forever. It's the only way to be safe. It wasn't supposed to be this way.

He read the message, but he didn't respond. So I called him. It took him many rings to answer. I was sobbing hard.

"What's up?" Brennan asked.

Not believing what I just heard, I asked back, "Did you not read my text?"

"Yeah, but I fell back to sleep," he answered.

I cried even harder. Then I hung up, turned on my shower, and got cleaned up and ready for church.

About a half hour later, I sent him another text.

> Me: I'm sorry. I didn't realize you felt absolutely nothing for me now. I understand now.

He answered 20 minutes later.

> Brennan: Knock it off.

Then 30 minutes later, I sent another text.

> Me: Thanks for confirming my decision to just take a shower and clean up instead of going to the hospital. No one is going to believe me anyway.

Brennan: Believe what?

Me: That I was assaulted.

Brennan: What? When? Who? How?

Me: Did you not read my message this morning? Why on Earth did you think I called you crying?

Brennan: I didn't pick that up from your message. I thought you were referring to your dream. You should absolutely go to the hospital.

Me: Too late. I'm freshly showered.

Brennan: That shouldn't matter. You should go anyway.

Me: I've endured enough in the last five years. No more.

Brennan: Who assaulted you? What happened?

Me: A date.

Brennan: Not reporting it/not going to the hospital is a mistake. He could do it to someone else.

Me: I have suffered so much for so many for

so long...I just can't suffer for what might
happen right now. I am tired of suffering.

Brennan: I'm sorry that happened
to you. Please go to the doctor and
tell them what happened. Begging
you.

Me: Why? Why is this important to you?

Brennan: Did you tell Mis? Your
family? Because it's the right thing
to do. Because he should at the
very least have the shit scared out
of him so that he never does it
again. And because women
are heard now. Don't wait
on it. Do it now.

Me: Women are not heard now. Nothing has
changed. Roe is GONE. Because of @#$%*!@
men. No one else knows. It's too early to
call/text. I will bear this myself. Well...almost
myself.

Brennan: I disagree. Metoo.
What is his name? I'd also
report him to the dating site,
provided that's where you met.

Me: I'm not doing this.

Brennan: I was going to look
into him and potentially call
your local police. I don't
understand your decision here.
This is not something to do
alone. So many women that
finally come forward all wish
they did so sooner. HE
COULD DO IT TO
SOMEONE ELSE TONIGHT!

# # # # #

After church, I texted my bestie, Mis. We talked through the events of last night and that morning. She asked if I wanted her to come over. I said "no," that I would be alright. There was only one person who could truly make me feel better at that moment.

I sat on the sofa for two more hours, deliberating what to do. And then I got up, put some peanut butter in a Kong for Finnegan, placed it in his little pen, and zipped it up after he entered. I grabbed my purse, locked the door behind me, and drove to Montgomery County.

I had no idea what I'd find when I got there...if anyone else would be there, if Lorelei would be there, if Clay would be there, or if even Brennan would be there. Neither did I know if he would even let me in when I knocked. But this was what my heart begged me to do.

When I arrived, I saw his car parked on the street. He was home...I let out a sigh. Then I stepped onto his porch and knocked on the door. No answer. I knocked again. Then I realized there was a doorbell. So I rang it. Within a minute, Brennan opened the door.

He opened his arms wide, and I dropped my purse and whatever else I was carrying on the floor. Tears flowed down like the Amazon, and I fell hard into his embrace. We stood there for at least two full minutes, holding onto one another.

"Jordyn," Brennan said, "it's OK. You are OK."

More tears.

"It's OK...you are OK."

And each time I started to release my grip on Brennan, he hugged me tighter.

Eventually, we let go.

"I'm sorry for showing up unannounced," I mustered. "I wasn't sure what or who I'd find here."

"Jordyn," Brennan replied, "I don't want you to ever feel like you can't come to my house...especially if you need help in a bad way. But if it's not an emergency, maybe just call first to make sure Clay isn't here."

"Right. And you are welcome at my place," I replied.

And for the next four hours, we talked...we reminisced about old memories...we laughed about stupid stuff...and eventually, we shared a meal that Brennan treated me to at the diner he frequented since his move out of our old apartment.

It was almost 9 p.m. when we got back to his place, and Finnegan was at home alone. I had to get going. We said our goodbyes with another long hug and more tears on my part. And then I ventured out into the pouring rain for the 1:20 drive home.

"Be careful, and text me when you get home," Brennan said. I nodded and made my way to the door.

When I got home, I saw that Brennan had sent a text message about five minutes after I had left.

Brennan: I should have offered for you to take my bed and stay. I apologize. Latent thinking...

> Me: Not at all. I couldn't have stayed because of Finn.

# # # # #

And with this, we began our dance again...sitting some out and cutting a rug from time to time. It was not an easy thing...this dancing. I mean, we both knew how, but the tunes were different now...and not as familiar. And it all boiled down to this: we had lived together for eight years, and saw each other and/or spoke every day for the 1.5 years prior to that. Since the break up, we struggled to communicate effectively...something we both thought we did well. Texting led to a multitude of misunderstandings and Hiroshima-style blow-ups. Phone calls were only moderately better, sometimes still ending in one of us hanging up on the other. Being face to face was truly the best scenario in terms of getting along and enjoying one another's company. The challenge was that Brennan just bought a money-pit of an old duplex in Montgomery County, and I was finally back "home" in Lancaster County. Neither of us was ready or willing to uproot again.

Beyond that, Brennan repeatedly had said over the course of our time together, "I have always been honest with you from the very beginning, Jordyn. I did not and do not want a relationship."

This, despite the fact that we had had one, and he seemed ok with that for the majority of our eight years together. His recent actions, oftentimes, seemed to indicate that he might still want and/or enjoy a relationship with me. He visited me many times at my new place in Lancaster; most of the time he responded to my texts and answered my calls; he spent quite a bit of money to go on my 50th birthday trip with me; and many times, he showed up for me when no one else did or could...at times when I really needed someone.

But, as much as he graciously welcomed me inside during this—my most desperate time of need—Brennan was not willing to grant me the grace I desired the most. I was not welcome whenever Clay was there, because according to Brennan, Clay was not ready, and likely would never be ready, to forgive me for the things that I had said over the past three or so years, as well as how I had said them.

To be fair, I had gotten loud when Clay would say bigoted, misogynistic, and generally offensive things to my ear. After hearing these things for three years, I had reached my breaking point. I could not stand by and allow the word "gay" to be used inappropriately one more time...I could not stand to hear about "snowflakes" and "soft" people...I could not bear to hear about how "stupid and immature" the girls were in his school. To my thinking, someone had to stand up to the naive yet dangerous spewings I heard come from a 16-, then 17-, then 18-year-old mouth. Someone had to share another viewpoint to the ones that hurt not only my ears, but my heart, my soul, my spirit. And I lost my shit on more occasions than I care to say, but I owned that. And I said as much to Brennan.

"Brennan, I am ready and willing to apologize to Clay for my part in this breakdown," I had said multiple times.

"Jordyn, I know my son, and he is not ready to talk to you," was the reply I received just as many times. "You should have been the adult in the room...you should not have responded the way you did."

I never said that I was perfect, and indeed I was not. And on a level or two, Brennan had a point. But was it not worth trying to speak to Clay now that he was 20 years old...in a last-ditch attempt to save what we both said was the best relationship we had ever had? The answer was apparently, *no. No, I'd rather risk losing you, Jordyn, than trying to repair the relationship between you and Clay. I'd rather not teach my son about forgiveness and that it's important to listen to someone's apology...even if you decide not to accept it. No, it's more important for me to save face with my son than give you the chance to right the wrongs you've done. No, Jordyn, you don't deserve that chance.*

What's more was that this staunch defiance on Brennan's part to my wanting to apologize to Clay reeked of Lorelei. That little phone conversation that she and I had last year was twisted up like a clown's balloon and shared with Brennan...even though she said she wanted it to be "confidential" and just between us. So she went directly back to Brennan and gave a convoluted and untrue version of what was actually said. That was why Brennan felt so betrayed by me...because he believed the tale his compulsively lying ex-wife spun without ever once asking me my side. And so Lorelei wanted me out of the picture for good, and in order to do that, she had to convince Brennan that I should never be allowed to speak to Clay again, for Clay's sake, of course.

While I was welcomed into Brennan's home that afternoon, I was not worthy of his grace; I was not worthy of Clay's grace, despite begging for both. And I supposed that was his prerogative. Maybe there was only one kind of grace that was truly freely and constantly given…one kind of grace that I did not have to earn…one kind of grace that no matter how badly I fell down in one way or another, I would always be granted.

And so I decided that I was going to stop trying to force a round peg in a square hole, and I would just let Brennan do whatever he was going to do. And if that didn't involve or include me, whatever we were would just die a slow, silent death.

18

Chapter 18: When Sinking, Look Up and Reach Out

My downstairs neighbor had known since I moved into my new apartment that I had been looking for full-time work, and she knew just how hard it had been to be able to find something. Marjorie knew I had had plenty of great first interviews...so great that I was told on at least a dozen occasions that I would get a second interview before the first one even ended. And she also knew that in more than half of those, I was ghosted for no apparent reason. Or that I was told the job was offered to someone else before I even got my shot at said promised second interviews. In other cases, women 15 years my junior were the hiring managers, and not a single one of them was interested in hiring someone who was more than qualified. Ahhhhh, yes. Ageism was alive and well.

So, one Saturday afternoon in April of 2023, Marjorie told me that she had mentioned me to the pastor at a church in downtown Lancaster. Marjorie worked on many housing initiatives with Pastor Mandy. And Marjorie thought we'd get along like peas and carrots, and that Mandy had a need for some office help.

So the next morning, I got myself up and went to visit Mandy's church. And because the average age of the congregation was 75 and there were about 30 people in the room, I stood out as the lone visitor, who was well-under age 75. Several members came to shake my hand and greet me. Mandy called me out during her "holy hellos" section of the service. And afterward, she came to greet me personally.

"Hi, I'm Jordyn," I began, "Marjorie's neighbor?" I wanted to draw the connection early and quickly, so she could tend to other congregants.

"Oh, yes, it's nice to meet you," the pastor began. "I'm glad you came to visit."

"I understand you might have a need for some office help?" I asked. "Here's a copy of my resume if you might be interested." And then I went into a bit of my professional and church background, as well as my volunteering that I had done at a neighboring nonprofit that served hot breakfasts to those who were hungry.

"Ok, yes," Pastor Mandy began. "If you've volunteered at Anchor, you are quite familiar with the population we serve. It's not for the faint of heart...but I can tell you already know that."

I nodded and smiled, acknowledging that what she said was true. As my new friend and love preserver, Jenny, had helped me discover, my passion was justice—justice for all people, regardless of creed, color, or cash flow.

Mandy and I agreed to touch base that week, and we did...a few times. And I learned that beyond being a church, this congregation also had an adult day center...and it gave Mandy the authority to serve the poor and downtrodden in the community.

The following Tuesday, I began my work as Mandy's part-time administrative assistant. I handled creating her weekly bulletins, preparing copies of the hymns each week, retrieving and sending the mail at the post office, and most importantly, receiving and vetting the visitors who showed up at the Center's doorstep each day. Some wanted to speak with Mandy...some NEEDED to speak with Mandy...many needed toiletries, clothes, snacks...some needed bus passes to get to job interviews or to a newly started job or to a doctor appointment.

And so I spent four hours a day, four days a week triaging whomever called the office or showed up in our little vestibule. And I immediately knew this was soul work...this was something I was born to do...this was something I was meant to do right at that particular point in my life...this was what God wanted me to do.

No, it was not covering the rent by any stretch, but it was paying the utilities and some of my credit card bills. And that was a help. But most importantly, it was helping me recover from the last job...the six-day job. And it was helping by Day 3.

On Day 3, Mandy walked with me to the post office, to show me where our box was so that I could collect the mail three days each week. On the six-block round-trip walk, Mandy greeted at least four folks who were without homes...folks who were living on the streets of Lancaster City. She called out to them each by name, unless they saw her first, in which case, they called out to her by name. She hugged, hi-fived, or gave a handshake to each, depending on their preference...and she already knew their preferences, because she **knew** them...she loved them.

I couldn't believe my eyes...here was a pastor who was not just talking the talk, but she was walking the walk...she was **living** the walk. It was utterly awesome and amazing to see the faces of people living on the streets light up when they saw her.

When we returned to the office, Mandy asked, "Jordyn, can you come into my office when you get a minute?"

My spidey sense went on high alert instantly. Anyone who has ever worked in an office knows that being called into the boss's office typically isn't a good thing.

"Sure, I'll be right there," I said and grabbed a notebook and pen.

As I entered, Mandy softly said, "Can you close the door?"

Oh, no...this can't be happening again! I thought to myself, blood pumping hard through my veins now. My mind raced to quickly recall if I had misspoken or done something wrong.

"I just wanted to tell you how amazing it is to have you here, Jordyn!" Mandy began. "You are doing a fantastic job!" My shoulders kicked the 1,000 pounds that were sitting on them to the floor. "I also wanted to ask if you think you'd like a few extra hours each week to do some case management work to help place some of our homeless folks into housing?"

"Whaaattt?!" I exclaimed in disbelief. "Are you serious? Absolutely!!! I would love to get into some meaty work here." I took a brief pause to backtrack. "Not that what I'm doing for the church isn't good work, but what I mean is that I'd love to do some social justice work!"

"Awesome, Jordyn!" Mandy replied. "This is going to be super. We need more boots on the ground when it comes to helping our unsheltered folks. And I think you're going to do a super job."

I smiled, thanked her, and went back to my desk out front. I plopped down in my chair with a ginormous smile on my face as I thought to myself, *Yes, Jordyn...this is exactly what you need right now...this is exactly what you need to be doing right now! Not just for you, but for those folks out in the streets with nowhere to go, not much to eat, and no one, save a few kind souls, to help them.*

What a night-and-day difference between my six-day boss, Andre, and Mandy. She was a genuinely good and kind person...she had to be in order to have earned the trust of folks on the streets. And we became fast friends...probably because it felt like we were so much alike. From our taste in authors, thinkers, and theologians to the way we thought about what justice means and who deserves it (the answer is everyone, by the way...everyone deserves justice). It wasn't long before Mandy invited me to her personal Friday night church gathering of friends whom she felt comfortable being herself around. I happily accepted. It felt so good to be included with someone who understood me on almost every level, and I was touched that she trusted me with her personal and private sides. Being a public figure like a pastor is a double-edged sword, where one little misstep in front of the wrong person can be a career-killing move. But Mandy knew she was safe with me.

Each day at the Center felt like a gift. Every single interaction taught me something about myself and my current situation of living on the last $6,000 I had to my name. I had just withdrawn the last drippings of the only remaining 401k I had. When that was gone, I was either going to be homeless or paying credit cards with other credit cards. I had a fair amount of open credit, but that was not an ideal situation or choice.

Every morning I made a conscious decision to keep putting one foot in front of the other...to keep applying for full-time jobs that I thought I would love or at least that would pay the bills plus some...to keep going.

And every morning, in the back of my mind, a little, ugly voice would whisper...

*"Jordyn...have you thought about what everyone is going to say when you run out of money? When you are homeless? When you have nothing? Have you thought about what everyone is going to say about the money you spent on travel, trinkets, treasures, and that tattoo, when you **should** have been saving? Have you thought about how the people who don't care for you at all are going to laugh their asses off at your choices and say that you deserve what you got?"*

And I would speak back to that judgmental jerk whom I named Jezebel...

"As a matter of fact, I have thought of all those things and more, Jezebel. And you know what? Not only is it none of my business what other people think about me, but also...I don't give a damn. I don't give a damn about any of those people who would dare to say those things about or to me. Those people don't care about me. And I don't have time for people who simply want to point out what I should have done in their mind's eye. Because they are not me. They have not lived through what I have lived through. They have not been disrespected, disregarded, and disappointed by people who should have loved them. And surely, they have not almost died twice on an operating table. And I owe none of them an explanation for my choices...because if none of them chooses to help me, if none of them chooses to see how I've been dealt several bad hands back-to-back-to-back, if none of them chooses me, then I do not have time for their worthless opinions about my life.

"In fact, I'm kicking the dirt off my sandals and moving on from those people. Somewhere, I will find a hospitable soul who will help me...a good Samaritan who can see that I have struggled, and he or she doesn't care about how I got to this place but simply wants to lend a hand up.

"So put that in your pipe and smoke it, Jezebel. Go bother someone else...or better yet, find something good to do with your time instead of making judgments about the lives of people in whose shoes you have not

walked one step. In short, Jezebel, go away. Go far, far, far away. You and your thoughts are not welcome here any longer. Peace out, Girl Scout."

Yes indeed, working with homeless folks in Lancaster City made me incredibly aware of and appreciative for everything I had, even if it was evaporating before my eyes. It also reminded me that God takes care of his own. And He does that through people like Mandy, through people at a dozen or so organizations in the city, through Love. And somehow, I still believed that Love would save the day for me as well. That way I could silence Jezebel's voice once and for all.

19

◠◡

Chapter 19: Pouring from an Empty Cup, but Listening with a Full Heart

Beyond Mandy's immense heart and gifts for working with and for the unsheltered and hungry, she was also incredibly gracious when it came to my working, living, surviving situation. I had been completely upfront and honest with Mandy when I started the job, telling her I was looking for and needed a full-time job and income. But I also told her that I would work evenings and weekends to keep doing her bulletins, music prep, and whatever else I could do from home on the weekends once I found full-time work.. She loved that idea, and was all in.

So when I told her that I had withdrawn the last of the money I had to my name, she said that I should come to her before I got to "empty"...and that we would figure something out.

As I sat in the chair across from her desk, with tears beginning to roll down my cheeks, she said, "Jordyn, you need to take care of you first. We'll figure out this stuff...that is no problem. But let's make sure you are good."

"Yes, Mandy," I began as I wiped my face with the back of my hand, "it's hard to pour from an empty cup."

We both nodded in acknowledgment. She smiled at me, and ended our conversation with this…

"Jordyn, it is my daily prayer that you find what you need to live. And it is also my prayer that we can continue the work we're doing here in the city…that somehow, God will work all this out."

I left her office, took the 13 steps back to my desk, sat down and thought to myself, "*What kind of boss, who truly appreciates you and your hard work, wishes the best for you…even if that means you would have to leave your current role with her?*" The answer, as it turned out, was *Mandy*. Mandy was that kind of boss…that kind of leader. A true leader. A true supporter. A true friend.

About a week after we had had the conversation about my financial resources coming to an end, Mandy told me that she had received a reference email from a job that I had applied to over a month ago. The job was an "donor engagement associate" role with a large Christian organization, based in Lancaster County, and the pay was well below what I was used to making, and below what I needed to pay all the bills. However, something was better than nothing, and if I wasn't offered "something" soon, I would effectively have "nothing" soon.

My own pastor told me she had received a similar email requesting a reference check the previous week, as well as a friend of mine and a former supervisor. The odd thing was this: I had never spoken a word to anyone at this organization…never had a phone call, never had a phone screen, never had an interview. Apparently, they believed in weeding out folks first via reference checks…even before they spoke with potential candidates. I had never experienced this sort of interview protocol before…and I wasn't sure what to make of it. I mean, I had applied more than a month ago, in reality, I could have already accepted another job, and they would have just wasted the time of all of my references. It seemed a bit "cart before the horse," but I guessed it worked for them.

About two hours after Mandy told me about the reference check, I received an email saying that the organization wanted me to interview over Zoom in about 1.5 weeks. I had to choose two days/time slots from a few that they provided. I did as requested.

In the meantime, I worked on refining my brainchild to get grant monies from Lancaster City or local churches or other nonprofits to hold an event in/around the block where the unsheltered and/or hungry folks congregated. I wanted to get something warm in their bellies, be it coffee or pizza or something else. And after several iterations of ideas, I also wanted to give them a voice...a voice that so often was heard solely by either Mandy or me when they came into the Center. Word about where to get help spread quickly on the streets, and people knew that Pastor Mandy would help if she could...if she had the funds to do so. And in the six short weeks since I began working there, I had seen more happy tears and heartfelt embraces between Mandy and people who were once homeless, imprisoned, jobless, addicted, or the like. Now, these folks had returned to the place–to the woman–who had given them a chance, who had given them a break, who had given them a hand up. She did not have a bottomless bank account, but she gave what she could from her discretionary fund every single day. She was not always able to help, but she listened with discernment, and she gave when and where appropriate.

And I witnessed the fruits of her generosity come through the doors. These were holy experiences to behold...lives that had been turned around with a little bit of money, and a ton of compassion and resource-dot-connecting. Mandy was changing lives in ways that no one could ever proportionately nor appropriately thank her for. But she didn't do it for the thanks...she did it for them. She did what she did because these folks were people...first and foremost. They were human beings, who deserved to be treated with dignity and respect, just because they existed.

The success stories that were told in her office were once stories of destitution, desertion, and dehumanization that had spun 180s. And because Mandy had given them the time and space to tell their ugly, heartbreaking, and down-and-out stories in the past, she was later gifted the privilege of hearing what her hard work and help had done to turn their lives around.

And so, as I thought more about my idea to solicit grant money from the City and donations from local food and coffee spots for a day to help those who were hungry and without shelter, it became increasingly clear to me that the folks on the streets should also have a voice that is heard. Their being heard was critical. We all have a story or two to tell about our lives, but we don't all have someone who is willing to listen, someone who thinks we have something valuable to say, someone who thinks we deserve to take up their precious time. So I began formulating what this event would be called, what it would look like, who we could partner with, and who from the community leadership should be there.

Come hell or high coffee, I was going to make something happen to fill empty cups and bellies with something warm, because I could rally the full hearts without problem.

20

❧

Chapter 20: Lagom

A few years ago, I began the practice of choosing one word on January 1 to focus on for the entire year, instead of making a New Year's Resolution that I would likely give up before I was 30 days in. Some of those words included: *joy, better, essential,* and *new.* For the year 2023, I chose the Swedish word, *lagom.*

I became a fan of Scandinavian traditions and customs a few years ago, when I discovered the Danish concept of *hygge.* And while the words don't always translate exactly into English, the concept of hygge is one of coziness and comfort, while lagom is about having "just the right amount...just enough"

Think about the children's story of *Goldilocks and the Three Bears.* Goldilocks tries out a few things in the bears' home–porridge, chairs, and beds. One bowl of porridge was too hot, one was too cold, and one was just right. One chair was too hard, one was too soft, and one was just right. And the bears' beds were exactly the same–too hard, too soft, and just right.

So for me, focusing on a year of lagom meant focusing on having, on achieving, on doing, on being enough. It meant having an income that was enough–not too little, not too much, but one that was just right.

One that covered my expenses. It meant achieving just enough tasks, just enough goals, just enough.

It meant eating, exercising, moving my body, sleeping, working, playing, socializing, and centering myself just the right amount. And it wasn't as easy as I had hoped.

For all the weight I had lost due to my brain tumor anxiety, I had gained all of it plus some back. And I was none too happy about that. I had proven to be a stress eater extraordinaire. I had been exercising quite a lot by playing pickleball on the regular, but since I stopped working at a local recreation center, my play time dropped off a cliff. My sleep had been awful since Brennan had split with me, and it had never really recovered. For almost 12 months, I had not had my regular full-time income. I had the socialization covered with church friends, old friends, and new friends. And centering myself and my soul was a work in progress, but good progress. I found that the better I slept, the more easily I could center, concentrate, and complete tasks. But good sleep was still an infrequent visitor, no matter how much I begged her to come each night. I still had hope that she would eventually set up permanent residence with me...but that was yet to be.

Still...lagom. Lagom. Lagom.

21

⌘

Chapter 21: Exiting Sugar, Entering Water

This story began when I was 12 years old with a beach ball being blown out of my grandpa's pool during a thunderstorm. Oh, how I wanted someone to save that ball for me. But alas, it was not to be.

Now, 38 years later, after consuming way too much sugar these past 520+ days back in Pennsylvania Dutch country, I am exiting my dependency on the evil white stuff. And hopefully, I will be able to enter the water in a few months, feeling comfortable in my own skin, albeit nowhere near where society says I should be, to wear the swimsuits I wore for my 50th birthday trip. Who knows, maybe a new beach ball will blow onto the scene. Maybe it will be a beach ball with some heft, some fortitude, some desire to stick around where the fun is. But if the next ball wants to keep on moving when the first gale-force wind blows through, so be it. I will let it go. Someday, I hope to find a ball that is up for more than a game or two of pool volleyball before it loses its air. But if no ball stands the test of Jordyn Osborne, that's fine. I will survive. I've proven to myself that I can do so many things on my own, by myself, for myself. And I will do the next things as well.

I am a water bearer, and I refused to drown.

138

I refuse to drown.

~ ~ ~ The End ~ ~ ~

Patriarchy, a Flooded Bathroom, and Unconditional Love

BONUS SHORT STORY
BY
JORDYN OSBORNE

But if I can't swim after forty days
And my mind is crushed by the crashing waves
Lift me up so high that I cannot fall
Lift me oh oh
Lift me up, When I'm falling
Lift me up, I'm weak and I'm dying
Lift me up, I need you to hold me
Lift me up, And keep me from drowning again
– "Flood" by Jars of Clay

Elsa slept hard, flat on her back, next to Jacob. The pain in her protruded belly made it hard to be comfortable in any other position. The 76-year-old woman was four months into a stage 4 liver cancer diagnosis, although the hard-working PA Dutch woman had no idea what stage 4 meant. She only knew she was losing weight everywhere, save her belly. Elsa had only completed the eighth grade in school...her father told her she needed to earn money for the family. As a nine-year-old girl, she was farmed out to other families to make their meals, care for children not much younger than her, and do the laundry. It's just how things were done in the farmlands of Southcentral Pennsylvania during the Great Depression. Education was not the priority for the parents of a young girl with a strong German work ethic and ice in her veins.

So a cancer diagnosis didn't scare Elsa very much...partly because she didn't understand how cancer worked and partly because she figured she would just tough it out like she had every other obstacle she had ever faced in her life. She would do whatever treatment the doctor recommended, she would force herself to rest, and she would be back to working around the house from sunup to sundown and mowing the neighbors' yards and trimming their shrubs in no time at all.

Elsa's belly hurt a lot of the time, but no one would ever know that. Elsa was what folks would call a "tough old bird," and that didn't really begin to describe how well she could handle pain. She never let on when the pain was high...she just endured it. It's what folks of German descent did, especially women born in the 1920s did...they endured all things.

# # # # #

When Elsa met Jacob, she was already engaged to another man. Truth be told, she found Jacob arrogant and full of himself. So she dismissed his advances at first. But after some persistence on Jacob's part, Elsa gave in and went on a few dates. In time, she learned she had misjudged him, and that Jacob was really a decent and kind man. Within six months' time, Elsa, then 18, had broken her engagement to Leon and accepted a proposal from Jacob, aged 21. He had just returned home from serving in Okinawa as an artillery runner.

Elsa and Jacob worked in the local cabinet factory for 10-12 hours a day, then they sold hand-picked strawberries out of the back of their station wagon, mowed yards for the neighbors who were older than them. They had just begun their lives as a married couple, and money was not plentiful for them. But like most PA Dutch folk in the area, they rarely rested until the sun had set, and were happiest that way.

The young couple began their life of toiling from sunrise to sunset as soon as they were married. In the first five years of married life, they had two sons, Adam and Peter. They rented a small house from Jacob's mother, Emilia, on a cute street in Jacob's hometown of Dallastown, PA. With Emilia's permission, they would fix up bits and pieces of the home from time to time, making it safer and cozier for themselves. They were both quite handy and mechanically inclined...so they made the only bathroom in the house a bit bigger, put in a new kitchen sink and cabinets they made themselves, made room for a linen closet, and extended the closets in both bedrooms. Shortly after Peter entered middle school, Elsa and Jacob sat down to discuss future plans to own a home of their own one day.

"Jacob, we are saving every possible penny we earn, except for our rent, utilities, the house fix-ups, and food," declared Elsa.

"Yes, this is very true, Elsa," Jacob said, nodding in agreement. In his mind, he acknowledged that the boys' clothes and furniture were mostly hand-me-downs from her sisters' children...or made by Elsa's hands. And the boys bought some of their own clothes from part-time jobs that they held at the local ice cream shop.

"I don't know about you, but I would like to own a home at some point," continued Elsa. "The question is do we buy an existing home, or do we build a new one?"

"Well," paused Jacob, "do you want to maybe ask my mother about buying this house? I mean, we're here, we like it, we've put a fair amount of work into it, and we have room enough for us and the boys at this point."

"Yes, but this is barely a three-bedroom house, Jacob," replied Elsa. "Peter's room is not much bigger than an oversized closet, and his clothes are stored under his bed or in the dresser in Adam's room."

"Well, this could be the first home we own, Elsa," Jacob posited. "We could buy another later. Let's see what Mother says, ok?" In times like these, Jacob wished his father were alive to provide some guidance and wisdom. But he had passed of pneumonia complications when Jacob was just seven years old.

Elsa took a deep breath and exhaled slowly. "Fine. We'll talk to her. Can you see when she is available? I can make dinner here."

Jacob made the arrangements with Emilia for dinner the following Friday evening. After work the day before dinner, Elsa stopped by a roadside stand for fresh vegetables, and then she hit the butcher shop for a fresh roast of beef. Emilia was a meat-and-potatoes kind of German, so Elsa had every intention of serving a delicious meal that Emilia would love when they made their ask regarding the house.

At 5:30 sharp on that Friday evening, Elsa put out a spread fit for a queen. She had made one of her specialties that she perfected as a young girl working in others' homes–beef pot pie. Now, this was not the Marie Callender's variety of pot pie...this was legit, hand-rolled dough squares, boiled in beef broth with the roast that eventually fell apart in the pressure cooker with quartered potatoes. Carrots, celery, and onions were added to the pot. Elsa had also made coleslaw, ambrosia salad, garden peas, and warmed dinner rolls with more butter than anyone should look at in one sitting, let alone consume. And for the main dessert, a chocolate wacky cake with granulated sugar icing. Elsa had just finished putting ice in the water glasses when Emilia knocked at the door.

"Hello, Emilia," answered Elsa, as she opened the door. "Please come in. I hope you are hungry." And with that, Emilia mustered a half-hearted smile for her daughter-in-law, and made her way through the entryway to the dining room where she saw Jacob already sitting at the head of the table.

"Hello, Mama," smiled Jacob. Emilia bent down to kiss her son on the cheek.

"Hello, Jacob," she returned. Then she sat down at the seat to his left. "Well, are there others coming? There is so much food here! Whoever is going to eat all this?"

Elsa grinned slyly, "No, it's just us. Adam and Peter are working tonight, and the leftovers will be our lunches and dinners for the next few days. As you know, we don't waste anything." And with that, she took her seat to Jacob's right, across the table from Emilia.

"Jacob," Elsa began, "would you please say Grace?"

Jacob and Elsa bowed their heads, while Emilia waited impatiently for Jacob to finish his chatter to someone with whom Emilia was never friendly.

"...Amen," finished Jacob. "Let's eat."

Elsa took the large ladle from the beautiful bowl in the middle of the table, and placed three heaping servings on Emilia's plate, then turned to

Jacob and did the same, and finally to her own plate. She then passed the smaller bowls of peas and coleslaw.

Emilia had had several meals prepared by Elsa, but this one was pretty extraordinary, and was now her favorite for certain. When paired with the coleslaw, buttered rolls, and peas, it was simply amazing. She even scooped herself another ladleful, of which Elsa took proud note.

"Are you enjoying the pot pie, Emilia?" Elsa inquired.

"Um, yes, it is good," Emilia matter-of-factly stated. Jacob also noticed how much his mother apparently enjoyed the meal...and that she did not gush about it, even though she went back for seconds on her own.

"Mother, Elsa and I would like to ask you something," Jacob began.

"Oh, what is it?" Emilia replied, her left eyebrow raised higher than the right.

"Well," Jacob paused, "we've been talking about buying a home...and we've been trying to decide if we should build a brand new home, or if we should buy an existing one." He stopped to let her react and/or respond.

"Ok," said Emilia, her head cocked to one side. "Are you asking for my advice?" She was clearly unsure of what he was asking.

"Actually, what we were wondering," Jacob said as he glanced over at Elsa, "is whether you'd consider letting us buy this house from you." Again, he took a pause. Then he continued, as he searched his stoic mother's face for the slightest clue as to her thoughts, "We've been paying down your mortgage on this place for about 10 years now, all the while giving you a bit of income to boot, and we like it here, so we wanted to ask if you'd consider selling the place to us for the remainder of the mortgage."

Two sets of eyes stared intently on the matriarch's face as she pondered the question just posed to her. Emilia took a sip of water before calmly and directly said, "Well, I suppose I could sell this house to you...but it would be for a good deal more than what's left on the mortgage," Emilia blurted out quite rapidly. "I mean, look at all the upgrades that have been done since you moved in here."

Incredulous, but trying to maintain her composure, Elsa began calmly but firmly, "Emilia, as you know, Jacob and I are the ones who have made all of these upgrades at our own expense and with your blessing. So, are we to understand that all of our blood, sweat, tears, and sacrifice will now COST us money? That you expect us to pay MORE for this house because it is worth more?"

"Yes, that is exactly what I'm saying," Emilia said without flinching or feeling, as she stared intently at Elsa, and never once so much as glancing at her son.

Elsa waited for five long seconds for her husband of 16 years to say SOMETHING in response to the craziness that just hit her ears...but alas, it did not come. So, she took it upon herself to say what had to be said.

"Emilia, that is the dumbest and most selfish thing I've ever heard, and I am not the smartest cookie in the batch, but by God, I know a raw deal when I hear one," Elsa rolled out the words like a red carpet. Pulling no punches, she continued, "Beyond that, Emilia, we will be moving out as soon as we find a new place to live. We have outgrown this one approximately 45 seconds ago."

Jacob said nothing, as he pushed the remnants of potpie broth around his plate to make like he was busy. He eventually got up, collected every-one's dinner plates and silverware, and took them to the kitchen. Elsa thought to herself, "*At least he had sense enough to do that much.*" When he returned to the table, he brought along dessert plates and a knife to cut the wacky cake.

Upon seeing what Jacob had in his hands, Elsa promptly got up and removed the cake from the table. Jacob and Emilia looked at one another in surprise. "I thought we were going to have cake, Elsa?" said Jacob.

"The cake is for the boys...they love it," replied Elsa. She paused for a brief moment, and continued, "I think dinner is over now." And with that, she left the room.

# # # # #

Eight short months following that fateful dinner, Jacob, Elsa, Adam, and Peter walked through the doorway to their brand new home, built to spec. The house was a gorgeous white brick rancher with a full base-ment, three full-size bedrooms, and two full baths...and it sat across the street and a few houses down from their old rental. Elsa thought it would be good to have a constant reminder of where they started...where they came from...and where they were now, thanks to hard work and good planning.

The boys grew up, married, and began their own lives in a few years...and Elsa and Jacob continued doing what they had always done: worked in the cabinet factory, mowed lawns, kept a spotless home, and socked away every dollar possible for a rainy day, enjoyed a very rare and occasional trip with friends, and bought a share of an eventual family hunting cabin with the boys in Northern PA.

Time did what time does...it ticked by at a constant pace when life is rather regimented and planned out. But things changed a bit when Emilia became sick. Elsa was 58 when Emilia, then 30 years her senior, became bedridden and unable to care for herself. Emilia had had two husbands, both of whom had passed. Her five sons, including Jacob, were local, but none of them were equipped and/or willing to do the compassionate care that was required for this frail, old woman. So Elsa did what had to be done...she put aside any past bad blood between Emilia and herself, and she went to Emilia's house daily for seven months. Elsa made food for and hand-fed her mother-in-law, bathed her from a large bowl of soapy water, changed and laundered her bedclothes, tended to all bed sores, and retrieved any special request from the old woman who was down to just three teeth and a few hundred white hairs on her head.

No one, including Jacob, has asked Elsa to do what she did for seven months, until Emilia's death. And no one, including Jacob, ever uttered a word of thanks to Elsa for all that she had endured...for all that she had to bury in order to endure. But Elsa never did it for the thanks or recognition...Elsa did the right thing, simply because it was the right thing to do. And because of love. For her husband. For his mother.

# # # # #

Elsa and Jacob continued living their fairly routine life...sunrise, coffee, toast, work at the factory, mow some lawns, sundown. They would visit with their granddaughters every few weeks, a trip to the race track to bet on the ponies (the youngest granddaughter, Stacy, really enjoyed going up to the window to place her $2 bets)—it was the one wasteful thing they allowed themselves—gambling at the track or at Atlantic City on a bus trip where they gave each senior $20 to spend in the casino. The oldest granddaughter, Jordyn, known as Jordy to family and close friends, never saw the appeal of gambling, nor did she understand why her grandparents worked so very hard for everything they had, then risked it on a slim chance of making more money. But in fairness, Elsa and Jacob hit the penny slots for a few grand on several occasions, and Jordy, and of course, Stacy, were thrilled for them.

The girls grew up loving their visits to Gram and Grandpa's house...whether for the annual Christmas cookie baking day, for Christmas Eve, for birthday dinners (beef pot pie was always the choice for both girls), or just to say "hi" for a few hours. It was a treat to walk into that white brick rancher...even if the first words out of Elsa's mouth were, "Hello, Suzie Q...looks like you've gained weight." Ahhhh, yes....one could always count on an old PA Dutch woman to call it as she saw it.

Years went by, Elsa and Jacob retired, and when Jordy got engaged, on her 30th birthday, Elsa couldn't have been happier. She loved Jordy's choice of a husband...probably because he was a "good eater." Braeden always finished up the leftovers and was never shy at the table. Braeden loved Elsa as well. They had settled on a long-ish engagement...14 months out, which gave them plenty of time to plan.

Then life happened, as it has a way of doing, and Jordyn threw a monkey wrench into the wedding plans...and at Braeden.

# # # # #

On Mother's Day 2003, Elsa and Jacob were invited to Adam and Gretchin's house for dinner. At the dinner table, Gretchin looked at her mother-in-law for a bit, as something looked off, but she couldn't quite place it. But within a few minutes, she saw it.

"Elsa, are you feeling OK?" asked Gretchin. "You look a bit yellow." And with that, Elsa let the cat out of the bag.

"Well, I've been having some stomach issues and just not feeling like myself," Elsa admitted reluctantly. Health issues, aches, pains, and the like were just things she had always held private...but now, Gretchin had pulled back the veil.

"Have you seen a doctor about this, Elsa?" Gretchin continued. By this time, Jordyn and Stacy were moving in for closer looks, which made Elsa a bit uncomfortable, but she knew they just wanted to help. Jordyn noticed the whites of Gram's eyes weren't so white...but definitely more yellow.

"Well, no...not for a while," admitted Elsa. "Do you think I should? I was there a few months ago about some stomach pains, but he said it was nothing."

Adam was looking hard at his mother now, too. "Mom, I think you should call the doctor first thing in the morning," he said. If you need me to take you, just let me know."

"Alright," agreed Elsa. "I'll call. You know...I wasn't feeling so great driving up here. Do you think you could drive us home?"

"Certainly," said Adam. "Stacy, do you want to drive your car down to Grandma and Grandpa's, so that I can ride home with you?"

"Sure, Dad," Stacy jumped in quickly. "Let me grab my shoes and keys."

Monday's doctor appointment led to another appointment, and another. The second one involved bloodwork, and the third appointment was at an oncologist's office. It wasn't long before the entire family knew that Elsa had been diagnosed with stage 4 liver cancer.

# # # # #

Two months later, Jordyn was getting her makeup done at a Clinique counter on a Friday morning at the mall. Her hair was swept up with pearled bobby pins, and by 4 p.m., she was gusseted up in a white dress with intricate bead applique in a Sunday School room at her church. Meanwhile, Braeden was in a tux somewhere, goofing off with his father and best friend. Grandma and Grandpa were helped into another room with Stacy for some photos, and then Jordyn entered for her pictures with her grandparents.

"Gram, you look so good today! I'm so glad the purple pantsuit fits you...it looks lovely!" gushed Jordyn.

Elsa broke into a broad, proud smile as she said, "Thank you, Jordy! I just wish you had gone with the original date next year so that I could feel better. But your grandpa and I are so glad to be here today." Jordyn smiled and held back tears that were coming on like the Johnstown Flood. Her Gram just didn't understand there would be no feeling better. That each good day was a true gift from God, and the next good day might very well be the last good day.

"Me, too, Gram...me, too," Jordyn said. "But we had a vacation already lined up for tomorrow, and we just decided not to wait and made it a honeymoon instead."

Jordyn's beloved pastor had cut his own family vacation short a day to come home and marry her and Braeden. And he did a spectacular job with the message, as she knew he would. The ceremony was at 6 p.m. by candlelight, as that was when Pastor Atticks could be there, and it went off without a hitch. A simple Italian family-style meal was served at a local restaurant. When a bride moves up a wedding by nine months, she makes some concessions...like the ones others were making for her. But there was no way under heaven that Jordyn would be married without her Gram present.

# # # # #

The next three months were rough on the entire family, especially since Elsa didn't truly understand what was happening to her body. And as the cancer had its way with her, dementia had set up shop in Jacob's hippocampus. No one really paid a ton of attention to what was going on with Jacob because of the pain Elsa was in and the obvious physical care that Elsa needed on the daily. She had deteriorated to the point that Stacy moved into her grandparents' home to help care for her at night, while working her professional job during the day.

Stacy was burning the candle at both ends, with an hour commute both ways and preparing meals for Elsa's ever-changing taste buds, slathering lotion on Elsa's alligator-skin legs—a nasty side effect of the chemo—and helping her to bathe. Although she was only 27, Stacy was whooped at the end of each week. Then the weekends brought on a full-time care schedule.

Jordyn and Braeden came over when they could, but they lived in the next county to the east, and Elsa told them not to come so much, as they were still newlyweds. Jordyn had a love-hate relationship with visiting her

Gram. She wanted to be there all the time, but physically, emotionally, and spiritually Jordyn was not built for seeing someone she loved more than life itself morph into a shell of herself. She took on all the emotions and placed them squarely on her heart...there was no other choice for an empath. So, she and Braeden visited two or three times a week...which was about all she could take.

Gretchin helped whenever she could as well, but Adam had a difficult time seeing his mother's body being ravaged and confined to a chair most of the hours in a day. No one had ever seen Elsa sit so much in her entire life. Peter and his wife lived down south, so coming north to help happened once every other month or so.

# # # # #

That night in September, four months into her diagnosis and treatment, Elsa slept hard on her back, after a particularly bad day of pain. Jacob lay next to her in their bed. Stacy sawed timber in their spare room. Somewhere around 1:15 a.m., Jacob got out of bed and made his way across the hall to the bathroom. A 79-year-old prostate made an uninterrupted night's sleep next to impossible. His side of the bed was closest to both the bedroom and bathroom doors. However, when he got to the bathroom, he panicked. There was water, three inches deep, covering the floor. The faucet at the sink was turned off, and so was one in the tub. He checked the toilet next, but it was not running either. So where did all this water come from? Jacob was flustered, and anxiety took hold of him. He had to fix this, but he didn't know how.

He went back to the bedroom, where Elsa was still sound asleep. He went over to her side of the bed and gently shook her left arm.

"Elsa," he said. "Elsa. There's water all over the bathroom floor, Elsa. I–I—I don't know what to do."

Elsa woke from her slumber, and Jacob repeated himself, "Elsa, there's water all over the bathroom floor, Elsa. I don't know what to do."

"Alright, Jacob, alright," she said. "Can you help me up?" She tried hard to focus her eyes. Finally, everything became clear. Jacob carefully sat Elsa up in the bed and swung her legs over the side of the bed. He bent down to put her slippers on.

"No, no slippers if there is water," Elsa said. Then she took his hand, and he led her out of the room, to the hall, where she had to take four steps to reach the bathroom entrance. Jacob walked into the bathroom ahead of her and began pointing at the floor.

"See, Elsa, there is water everywhere," Jacob cried. "I don't know where it came from...it's all over."

Elsa blinked a few times and looked all around the 3x6 bathroom floor. Despite the 8 out of 10 pain level that she was in, she grabbed a towel off the rack on the wall and used the bathroom vanity to carefully get herself down on all fours to mop up the floor. Elsa shook her head slowly and ran her hand over the bone-dry bathroom floor, then she looked up. She could see how distraught Jacob was.

"Can you fix it, Elsa?" Jacob asked. "Can you make it better?"

"I will handle it, Jacob," Elsa said. "Just please step out into the hallway so that I can take care of it." And Jacob did what his wife asked, and she began to make large circles with the bath towel all across the floor. After a minute, she stopped, threw that towel into the tub, and asked Jacob to toss her the second one on the rack. He did just that, and as she lifted her head to look at him, Elsa saw Jacob's face begin to brighten. *"It's working,"* she thought to herself. So she continued wiping up the floor, and inched her way toward the door frame. She tossed the second "wet" towel in the tub and used the tub and towel rack to get herself up. Jacob had already gone back to bed and was fast asleep...he was exhausted from the trauma.

Elsa, too, made her way back to their bedroom, using walls, the foot of the bed, and furniture to steady herself as she went. When she finally got to her side of the bed, she flopped her bottom down and sat there for a minute or two, collecting her strength. While she recovered, waiting for the right time to try to swing her legs up onto the bed, she began to softly hum a song to herself. Her grandbabies loved when she would hold them in the pleather orange rocking chair in the basement and sing the little tune when they were young. Then somehow, the words ever-so-softly left her lips:

"She'll be coming round the mountain when she comes
She'll be coming round the mountain when she comes

She'll be coming round the mountain, she'll be coming round the
mountain
She'll be coming round the mountain when she comes
She'll be driving six white horses when she comes
She'll be driving six white horses when she comes
She'll be driving six white horses, she'll be driving six white horses
She'll be driving six white horses when she comes
Oh, we'll all go out to meet her when she comes
Oh, we'll all go out to meet her when she comes
Oh, we'll all go out to meet her, we'll all go out to meet her
We'll all go out to meet her when she comes..."

And with that, Elsa took a deep breath, heaved her lead-like legs up onto the bed, and drifted back to sleep. Her heart and mind, now comfortably resting, knowing her husband was at peace for the night.

When morning broke, Jacob tried to rouse his wife, but to no avail. Elsa had gone on a ride with six white horses...but she'll be waiting for everyone to come out and meet her.

Thank you for coming along on this journey that has been the last five years of my life. It's been quite a ride. If you've enjoyed my story, please share it with a friend or anyone who might also enjoy it.

Wishing you compassion, mercy, and wisdom,

~~The Water Bearer